"My husband, and our father, saw the need to create and developed healthy food for pets. We are proud of his contributions, and appreciate the recognition he deserves in this book. This book wonderfully captures the beginning and evolution of a great company that builds upon John Saleen's desire to improve the pet industry. He sought to increase awareness and accessibility for better health care for everyone's pets. We are grateful to the authors for sharing this story."

- The Saleen Family: Mrs. Evelyn Saleen, Steve Saleen, Mike Saleen and Robyn Saleen Blue

"A confirmation of how great things can happen when a company hires the best and brightest people and establishes a culture that allows them to propel the organization. The passionate culture was not limited to employees; it expanded to the trusted outside talent that provided services to the company. A wonderful example of great American optimism and can-do spirt!"

-Gerry Leukam, *Vice President - Design Services, The Weitz Company*

"The authors have been gifted with the ability to take the complexity of what a successful business has done and translate it into an easy to understand template that other budding entrepreneurs can use and apply for their endeavors. Within the pages of this inspiring read, she captures the cultural spirit of this ground-breaking company that engaged the hearts and mind of their employees and partners to achieve what was at first, unthinkable. A highly recommended read."

- Paul Butler, *Los Angeles Area Chamber Board of Directors*

"Being part of the explosive growth of natural health food for pets was one of the biggest joys of my professional career. Not only did we get to bring a small unknown dog food company to international prominence, we did it with a unique direct marketing program that was new to consumers. Instead of relying on traditional mass media advertising, we did it by connecting with consumers and through this loyalty, we built our business one bag at a time."

-Edmund Brown, *Former Owner of Nutro*

"A riveting and fascinating look at how one small company using desire, passion and the law of attraction became a driving force in the marketplace. A blueprint for companies and CEO's who wish to establish a win-win culture within their organization."

- Jerry MacDaniel, Author-*Channeling the Mothership*

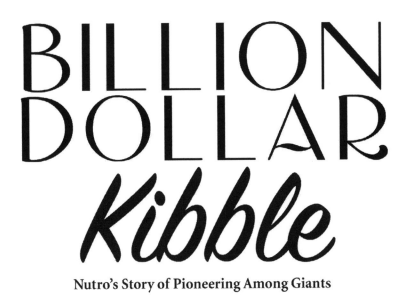

BILLION DOLLAR
DOLLAR
Kibble

Nutro's Story of Pioneering Among Giants

Christie Cooper and Mary Hooks

Table of Contents

FOREWORD

We learn from each encounter we have throughout our lives. At the age of fifty, I took a leap of faith that would later become one of the proudest moments in my life.

This leap of faith happened during the 1970s. I was an outside sales representative working at a distributor of hard-good pet supplies called Lee Mar. I knew *of* John Saleen, as he was the then-owner of Nutro. I intentionally sat by him at lunch while attending the World Wide Pet Show Association in the mid-1970s. The conversation I ended up having with him would change the trajectory of my life.

As I look back over the years, I realize that my colleagues and I didn't do anything very complicated; we just successfully developed an entrée that was hard to say no to. We listened to what the consumer wanted and told them that our product would solve their pets' problems. I can't recall a store that we did not get our products into.

This is the amazing tale of how a company that was purchased for $300,000 in 1976 went on to be sold for over *two billion dollars* in

2009—and the people who helped make that happen. I am excited to be a part of this book's journey, having Christie Cooper and my daughter, Mary Hooks, author the story of and for all of us who were a part of this amazing adventure.

Good Selling Tiger!

Ed Brown

DEDICATED TO

Inspired by a poem written by Robert Frost in 1916, Nutro Products used the motto "the road less traveled" to motivate a sales team to realize that selling one bag of a food at a time would lead to success in the retail industry. Most importantly, the company changed the lives of pets and influenced the way pet parents would purchase their dog and cat food.

Two roads diverged in a yellow wood,
And sorry I could not travel both
And be one traveler, long I stood
And looked down one as far as I could
To where it bent in the undergrowth;

Then took the other, as just as fair,
And having perhaps the better claim,
Because it was grassy and wanted wear;
Though as for that the passing there

Had worn them really about the same,

And both that morning equally lay
In leaves no step had trodden black.
Oh, I kept the first for another day!
Yet knowing how way leads on to way,
I doubted if I should ever come back.
I shall be telling this with a sigh
Somewhere ages and ages hence:
Two roads diverged in a wood, and I—
I took the one less traveled by,
And that has made all the difference.

~Robert Frost

THOSE WHO TOOK THE
ROAD LESS TRAVELED . . .

In Memory of

Bill Sandifer	George Buttes	Jeff Petersen
Bubba Green	Haig Kanosian	Kenny Owen
Dan Provenzano	Howard Hood	Chuck Davis
Debbie Markson	Jason Forward	John Calfas
Don Taffy	Linda Adolph	Larry Waranka

Still in our midst

Aaron Schmidt	Hardy Frink	,Michael Amador
Adrian Hernandez	Harold Gillard	Michael Ferraro
Adriana Valencia	Haydee Woody	Michael Gagne
Agustin Romero	Hazel Paguio	Michael Green
Akruti Pathak	Heather Gillespie	Michael Justice
Al Cline	Heather Huertas	Michael Manjarrez
Al Treccia	Hector Hernandez	Michael Rivard
Alan Colna	Hector Martinez	Michael Romero
Alejo Valez	Helen Sherry	Michael Rosick
		Michael Scott
Alex Solis	Helena Keck	Michael Usery
Alfredo Sotelo	Ines Feijoo	Michelle Dickerson
Alicia Cac	Inga Rodriquez	Miguel Gutierrez
Alissa Sablan	J. Change	Mike Bioini

Allen Arias	J. Tomey	Mike Carr
Alma Avena	J.R. Winkler	Mike Chandler
Alvaro Manzo	Jack Hahn	Mike Gagne
Andrea Raich	Jack Murray	Mike Green
Andrew Budrow	Jack Zubritzky	Mike Hale
Andrew Hogan	Jackie Bulger	Mike LeVan
Andy Crawford	Jackson Dering	Mike Munoz
Andy Crowell	Jade Dominique	Mike Poss
Andy Epping	James Kilton	Mike Satterwhite
Andy Faessler	James McClernon	Mitch Finn
Angela Regan	James Simplot	Moises Negrete
Angela Weir	James Talley	Mynor Peralta
Anita Revelles	James Verdon	Myrna Lamera
Anthony Giudice	Janie Klatt	Nancy Cantwell
Anthony Quinn	Jasmine Atar	Nancy Carr
April Palacious	Jason Bailey	Nancy Heiss
Ariel Angeles	Jason Cohen	Neil Borne
Art Munoz	Jason Desilva	Odette Coco
Arthur Peyser	Jason McCullagh	Odette Kirby
Arturo Mejia	Jason McGull	Olber Tadeo
Austin Newton	Jason Montgomery	Onyango Edwards
Bac Nguyen	Jan Thydean	Ora Rittiket
Barry Curtis	Javier Pulido	Oscar Miranda
Becky Soto	Jeanine McDonald	P. Weisbery
Beth DeLeon	Jeff Barton	Pam Falcone
Beth Emhoff	Jeff Hicks	Patricia Koonter
Bill Barry	Jeff King	Patricia Timmons
Bill Fitts	Jeff Lysak	Patrick Hamill
Bill Green	Jeff Mount	Patrick Murphy
Bill McElhaney	Jeff Nashar	Patti Boehm
Bill Morat	Jeff Phillips	Paul Hoeft
Bill Rahn	Jeff Postma	Paul Leaming
Bill Sandifer	Jeff Rachu	Paul Pierson
Bob VanColt	Jeffrey Williams	Paul Sopsic

Brad Cochrane	Jel Cardoza	Paul-Eric Boulanger
Brad Plein	Jennifer Ketola	Pedro Gonzalez
Brandi Gerhardt	Jennifer Moffitt	Pedro Gonzalez
Brandon Due	Jeremiah Cooper	Peggy Pleins
Brenda DuBois	Jeri Gagne	Peggy Pennington
Brenda Neidlinger	Jerry Beaudion	Pepito Canonizado
Brent Humphrey	Jerry Gagne	Pete Shepherd
Brett Davis	Jerry Harding	Peter Trevino
Brian Avants	Jerry McDaniel	Pierre Gadbois
Brian Bogart	Jerry Serrano	RaChelle Baca
Brian Cunningham	Jerry Sicherman	Rafael Magallon
Brian Gay	Jerry Villanueva	Rafi Kalachian
Brian Records	Jerry West	Ralf Klingebiel
Brian Smith	Jerry Young	Ralph Pena
Bruce Voss	Jessica Sanchez	Ramiro Sanchez
Bryan Allen	Jessie Oakley Slaton	Ramon Napoles
Buddy Rehkopf	Jesus Torres	Ramona Ramire
Cameron Houser	Jill Blaylock	Randy Hubbard
Cameron Passey	Jill Hunt	Raquel Hernandez
Carl Mokosak	Jim Belser	Ray Navarro
Carlos Contreras	Jim Gorrell	Raymond Zumfelde
Carlos Diaz	Jim Kepler	Rebecca Mekee
Carlos Rivera	Jim Nerihs	Renee Ganey
Carmel Vargas	Jim Simplot	Reyes Garcia
Carol Linkins	Jim Wheeler	Ricardo De La Cruz
Carol Strode	Jimmy Misiuk	Rich Zanetti
Cesar Mendoza	Jo Hollingsworth	Richard Ueltxchi
Chad Calhoun	Joan Dillon	Rick Celentano
Chad Cooper	JoAnn Collins	Rick Petts
Chad Maddox	Joaquin Munoz	Rik Clark
Chad Polski	Joe LoCicero	Rob Glenn
Charles Keating	Joe Siciliano	Rob Johnson
Chris Dempsey	Joel Cleveland	Rob Lawson
Chris Dennis	Joel Dillard	Rob McCarthy

Chris Kenady	Joey Rogers	Robaab Amjadi
Chris Smith	John Bennett	Robert Beatty
Chris Wilburn	John Cariglio	Robert Esquivel, Sr.
Christelle VanSteenkiste	John Eishenheimer	Robert Glenn
Christian Hoehn	John Henderson	Robert Hutter
Christian Nourry	John Hooks	Robert Lawson
Christie Cooper	John Luisi	Robert Nailon
Christina Juarez	John Martin	Robert Rabichuk
Christine Carrion	John Rivera	Robert Vanas
Christopher Dempsey	John Ruter	Robert Young
Chuck Lata	John Senich	Roberto Ruiz
Cinda LaBaron	John Vanaken	Robin Florio
Cindy Johnson	Jorge Ramirez	Rogelio Rabaan
Cindy Vasquez	Jose Colunga	Roger Clark
Claudia Estevez	Jose Esparza	Roger Hyde
Clayton Mariotti	Jose Noelmestas	Roland Caramagna
Clifton Foster	Jose Segura	Romy Francisco
Colin Lundrigan	Joyce Verham	Ron Ong
Conny Versendaal	JR Winkler	Ron Sanderson
Corinne Blair	Juan Puentes	Ronald Vinhateiro
Corey Lanier	Juan Ramirez	Rosa Maneri
Cory Parsons	Juan Villegas	Rosalie Garcia
Craig Lammers	Kate Sterling	Ruben Felix
Craig Saling	Kathryn Ricks	Rudy Leschke
Damian Cooper	Kathy Garrison	Russ Lowell
Dan Calkins	Kathy Lambert	Rusty WOrstell
Dan Fortuna	Kayleen Taylor	Ruth Kennedy
Dan Gramp	Keith Elrod	Salvador Ramos
Darcy Hagen	Keith Sweet	Sam Shum
Daren Blais	Kelly Burns	Samuel Galdamez
Daren Simmons	Kelly Donohue	Sandra Perez
Darlene Kurtzweil	Kelly Wucherpfennig	Sandy Hayes
Dave Horton	Ken Bush	Sandy Kasten
Dave Kelly	Ken Nowak	Saul Acosta

Dave King

Dave Kravis

Dave Martin

Dave McDonald

Dave Orr

Dave Otting

Dave Traitel Jr.

Dave Weigel

Davia Frias

David Ivester

David Nye

David Silver

Deb Wilson

Debbie Evans

Debbie Stampley

Debby Davis

Deby Lu

Denise Montenagro

Denise Vega

Dennis Pollard

Dennis Sullivan

Dennis Warnke

Dennoy Ly

Dewey Armstrong

Dewey Long

Diana Romero

Dirk Litten

Don Carlson

Don Hoang

Don Law

Don Pabisz

Don Williams

Donald DeLaCerna

Donald Young

Ken Purchase

Ken Wiechman

Kendle Newson

Kevin Hunt

Kevin Keller

Kim Douglass

Kim Goldberg

Kim Mailloux

Kim Mann

Kim Mitchell

Kim Scott

Kimberly Foutz

Kip- BT West

Kirk Impecoven

Kirk Olischefski

Kirk McClaren

Kristy Murphy

Kui Kawata

Kurt Gergle

L. Akinyemi

L. Miranda

Ladd Hardy

Lance Watkins

Lanny Bartlett

Larry Abramovitz

Larry Glick

Larry Martinez

Laura Johnson

Laurie Hagelis

Leigh Garry

Lenore Bartlett

Leo Pinal

Leslie Bell

Leticia Gallegos

Scott Abrams

Scott Haff

Scott Huntley: BT West

Scott Keller

Scott Reinhardt

Scott Springfield

Scott Warwick

Sean Heisler

Sergio Barios

Sergio Milia

Shane Allgood

Shane Giardino

Shane Niles

Shannon Seiler

Sharie Fontana

Sharon Machlik

Sharon Morton

Shawnda Navarro

Skip Kroeger

Stacey Hudson

Stan Goodman

Stan Grumbeck

Stanford Gilbert

Stephen Lindsay

Stephen Tait

Steve Buccelli

Steve Buzzi

Steve Callahan

Steve Chan

Steve Hallford

Steve Nelson

Steve Reed

Stu Ray

Sue Wei

Donnell Sablan	Lewis Whelchel	Sue Yolman
Doug Amdur	Lia Rivadeneyra	Susan Lutz
Doug Sterling	Lilia Garza	Susan Torres
Douglas Fischer	Lisa Cromwell	Susan West
Earl Smith	Lisa Lambrakis	T. Coombes
Edvin Tiguila	Lisa Laughlin	Tamara Cerven
Edward Mittwer	Lisa Miller	Taryn Herder
Eli Ellis	Lisa Pierce	Ted Walker
Elisas Cornejo	Lisa Steltemeier	Teresa Hill
Elizabeth Ramirez	Lizbeth Sanchez	Terry Halteman
Emilio Rivera	Lori Johnson	Terry Manheim
Enrique Santamaria-Rivera	Lori Joyce	Terry Thomann
Eric Dwyer	Lori Wojack-Thomas	Theresa Johnson
Eric Partenheimer	Louis Mouton	Thomas Flayhan
Erica Flores	Luca Bianchini	Tiffany Tuck
Erin Lee	Lucas Bosco	Tim Gallagher
Erin Patterson	Ludy Frew	Tim McMahon
Errol Brown	Luis Gonzalez	Timothy Scoullar
Esaul Orozco	Luis Raya	Timothy Treadwell
Evelyn Mendoza	Luis Santillan	Tineke Timmermans
F. Malekzadeh	Lyle Starr	Tm Howell
Fabrizio Spena	Lynn Driscoll	Todd Hyatt
Faustino Baena	Lysa Richards	Tom Cameron
Felipe Castillo	Manuel Almaguer	Tom Caramanica
Felix Hernandez	Marcelino Solis	Tom Kapocious
Fernando Del Campo	Marcella Perez	Tom Latoza
Flavio Ortiz	Marco Ramirez	Tom Serizawa
Francesca Waldron	Margaret Goodall	Tomas Rivas
Francisco Granados	Margie Moss	Tony Miller
Francisco Herran	Maria Barbosa	Tracy Hall
Frank Frias	Maria Castro	Tracy Morrison
Frank Hon	Maria Sanchez	Trevor Snelling
Frank MacMillan	Marie Kinder	Troy Firth

Fred Corbett

Fred Kroeplin

Fred Smith

Fredy Gomez

Fritz Condon

Gail Riffel

Gary Crosslin

Gary Lentz

George Briscoe

George Iqueda

Gera Herrera-
Sepulveda

Gerald Toussaint

Gerardo Hernandez

Gerard Kearns

Gerry Leukam-
Ibberson

Gino Diaz

Gordon Ross

Greg Acari

Greg Braithwaite

Greg Hayden

Greg Hutsell

Greg Mandel

Greg McElhaney

Gregorio Espinoza

Gus Baltabois

Gustavo Renteria

Hannon Namahoe

Hans Sleeger,

Marina Murillo
Sanchez

Marina Scholefield

Mario Lomeli

Mark Anderson

Mark LaCorte

Mark Larson

Mark Mount

Mark Paepke

Mark Reed

Mark Sorge

Mark Wareing

Martha Garcia

Martha Puente

Martin Young

Martyn Bee

Mary Hooks

Maryline River

Mat Pira

Matt Chisolm

Matt DeFreitas

Matt Dixon

Matt Kimmel

Matt Thomas

Matthew Lorfing

Megan Carbonne

Melissa Colpitts

Melissa Done

Meredith Taggert

Mia Lugo

Troy LaBranche

Troy Lebo

Tynna McChesney

Valerie Buford

Valerie Ybarra

Veronica Rumishek

Vicki Hargis

Vickie Akau

Victoria Chavez

Virginia Diaz

Ward Reynolds

Warren Montgomery

Wayne Bernal

Wayne Renfrew

Wayne Siegrist

Wes Boots

Wes Wagner

Whitney Piatkowsky

Woody Austin

Xavier Muratella

Yari Romandia

Yolande Hill

Yuki Morisawa

Zeferina Vidrio

ACKNOWLEDGMENTS

Billion Dollar Kibble was inspired by all those who—as we often said at Nutro Products—"took the road less traveled." Everyone at Nutro used this saying to refer to the strategy that we did *not* use, instead favoring the one that certainly took more fortitude. Without the dedication of every individual who worked for and with Nutro, none of this would be possible. We pay special remembrance to James Spratt, whom numerous authors have recognized as someone who saw a niche and made a pet food that would revolutionize the way people would feed their dogs—forever.

A special heartfelt acknowledgment goes out to Steve Saleen, whose drive and passion has impacted two industries: pets and cars. Steve's insights invaluably gave shape to the true beginnings of our book. Mike Saleen was instrumental as well in the book's development. Since the passing of their father, John, both brothers and their sister, Robyn, graciously shared memorabilia and stories with us.

Another name that must be recorded in the history books of pet food is Herben Serois. Back in 1931, Herben was the *original founder* of The Nutro Dog Company. Little is known or written on Herben, and it has been painstaking—yet incredibly rewarding—to dig up the information that we have on this entrepreneur.

Finally, were it not for Dave Traitel and Ed Brown taking a *leap of faith* and buying the company, none of us would have the extended family that we do today.

INTRODUCTION

The company formerly known as The Nutro Dog Food Company—for which we worked for twenty years—has been privately held and independently owned since 1931. A man named Herben Serois founded this obscure, humble, yet remarkable business, which has always been based on creating a type of health food for dogs. By formulating a product with qualities vastly different from their competitors, Nutro became a true icon in the pet industry.

"Selling one bag at a time" was another expression that members of the organization fondly used to express the great lengths to which individual people would go to promote Nutro Products. Ultimately, it created a movement within the pet industry. The company's competitors considered Nutro's associates to be almost cultlike in their faith toward this approach. In fact, these employees believed so much in what they were selling that the only option for anyone was to feed their pets "The World's Best Dog Food." And these are the very people who have helped us tell this story.

When we set out to write this book, we were overwhelmed by the warm reception and encouragement we received from our colleagues. From the first planning meeting we had, to contacting John Saleen's children—Steve Saleen, founder of Saleen Mustangs; Mike Saleen, retired deputy district attorney; Robyn Saleen, college professor—and then speaking to our Nutro family members, we realized that the timing could not have been more perfect. People told us, "I'm delighted to hear that somebody wants to record this history," to, "I thought about doing that ten times myself, but I never had the time," and "Yes, I am happy to participate!" Some told us it felt like a good therapy session to reminiscence about the company. This process has given us the wonderful opportunity to connect with the colleagues that we consider family—many of whom we'd not spoken to in years. We wanted each person to share their recollections and favorite stories, and help us understand their view on what made the culture so special—and what drove Nutro into the hearts and minds of our loyal pet parents.

This book aims to give other entrepreneurs the inspiration to achieve success and greatness in their right. It will also share the insights of the strategies and culture that allowed a solopreneur to launch a company into the hearts and minds of millions of consumers.

CHAPTER 1: PAW PRINTS ON MY HEART

"If there are no dogs in Heaven, then when I
die I want to go where they went."

–Will Rogers

There was a bleak and ominous weather forecast that day in Cheyenne, Wyoming—the type of day that would keep most people indoors and attached to their wood-burning stoves to ward off the dampness and chill. But there was no way the young newlyweds from California were going to stay home. Howard and Christie were high school sweethearts who married as young adults—really, still teenagers. After Howard graduated high school, he spent a semester at the local community college. However, he felt this path would not lead him toward his ultimate goal of becoming a Los Angeles deputy sheriff, so he joined the Air Force. After graduating basic training, he found himself stationed in Cheyenne. Shortly after, he married Christie, and she moved back with him. Leaving behind sunny days and great weather year-round in Southern California, they set off to Bushnell, Nebraska, in hope of selecting their newest family member.

While exiting Interstate 80, the already dark skies seemed to grow black. The young couple had chosen to watch *Children of the Corn* the previous evening, and they suddenly felt as though the movie were coming to life. The cryptic directions they received took them through a small town surrounded by fields of corn so tall and lush they seemed impenetrable. After driving through the tranquil community without seeing a soul, the directions took them to the front gates of a cemetery at the edge of town. Evidently this was the resting place for many of the town residents who had long since passed away. The dirt-lined road curved up toward a rustic barn at the top of a hill. "Hey, babe, do you think we should really be going this direction?" Christie asked with a lump in her throat. Howard, eager to reach their destination, replied, "Quit worrying! And stop thinking about the movie you just watched. Everything will be fine." With their hearts in their stomachs and dark clouds overhead, they continued on their trek.

They guessed that since it was Sunday, perhaps most townspeople were churchgoers and were still worshipping. Howard placed their truck in gear and slowly ascended the hill. As they neared the end of the cemetery, Christie pointed to the silhouette of a large dog. Highlighted by the morning sun, a black Labrador with a masculine jawline and broad chest sat rock steady as it watched them approach. Barking loudly, the dog alerted the farmhouse residents of the approaching strangers. Moments later, two young children appeared behind the black Lab. The couple breathed a sigh of relief as they eagerly got out of their truck. Nearby, fifteen black-and-yellow, somewhat pudgy puppies scampered around with the two children. Howard and Christie were happily mauled by fifteen possibly new family members.

Howard fell in love with a Dijon mustard–colored female Labrador. At seven weeks old, she had one more week before she could accompany them home to their apartment. Christie waited anxiously for their "baby" to come home—and once she arrived, they settled on the name Buffy. They took Buffy everywhere with them, and as far as they were concerned, Buffy was not "just a dog." She was truly the couple's first child before they started their human family.

Several years later, the couple moved back to California and expanded their family with the birth of their daughter. Buffy was mesmerized by this new infant, to whom everyone was paying so much attention. Sniffing and licking the baby quickly became commonplace. By the time the couple's daughter began to walk, Buffy was the perfect training aid for standing and walking. Buffy never objected and was always compliant, despite the occasional ear or tail tug as their child struggled to maintain her wobbly stance.

Howard and Christie, now approaching their thirties, awoke one morning to realize Buffy did not seem quite right. Her enthusiastic morning kiss and snuggle went missing as she lay on her bed. The couple, fraught with concern, called in sick to work and took Buffy to the local vet. The vet gave a thorough examination and concluded that Buffy needed an ultrasound on her abdomen—which he was not equipped to conduct. Christie did some quick research as to who in Southern California was the best canine internal medicine specialist, and found a medical group in Santa Monica whom they contacted at once.

A very empathetic receptionist greeted the couple and took down the necessary information. The staff set up an examining room with the latest technology, ready to receive Buffy. While examining her, the vet told the couple, "Buddy, my black Lab, loved to duck hunt—which he did up until his arthritis kept him out of the field. I was lucky to have him 'til he was fifteen." His story comforted the couple and gave them confidence that he would provide the best care and compassion while trying to save their beloved family member.

The vet went on to say how stoic dogs can be. Even in Buffy's final moments, she never complained; she simply thumped her tail happily as she lay on the examination table. There was no limit that day to the amount of money the couple would have spent to save her. Unfortunately, she was in final stages of liver failure. Buffy was their first family member and she was in their lives for twelve years. They remember her fondly, referring to Buffy as "The world's best dog!"

Most people can easily recall the time they brought a new pet into their household—or the time their pet found them—or even the difficult end-of-life decisions that some people are forced to make. Whether the event is joyous or sobering, one thing remains the same: *Pets are our family*. We bestow upon them human traits and emotions. We treat our dogs and cats as if they are our children. Spending is at an all-time high for pet products, especially for pet foods.

And that's where our part of the story begins.

CHAPTER 2: THE GENESIS: FROM THE UK TO THE USA

"Do not follow where the path may lead. Go instead where there is no path and leave a trail."

Exact author unknown

Let's travel back in time to just after the turn of the nineteenth century. Shipping had become the lifeblood of the world's economy, connecting manufacturers to customers and allowing the exchange of goods cross-continentally. On one such transatlantic trip, James Spratt (Figure 1), an American inventor and entrepreneur, set sail from the United States for England around 1850.

Figure 1: Photo of James Spratt, unknown year.

An electrician by trade, Spratt—an Englishman of seemingly endless ingenuity—earned numerous patents for his efforts in hermetic sealing, lightning conductors, cattle feeding, and "Meat Fibrine Dog Cakes." The last of these revolutionized the way people all over the globe fed their dogs. The product, shown in Figure 2, was Spratt's foray into commercially prepared pet food.

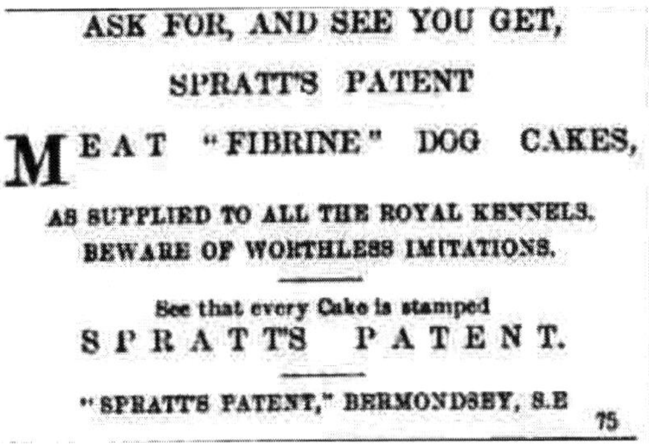

Figure 2: Spratt's Fibrine Dog Cakes advertisement.
Newspaper image © The British Library Board. All
rights reserved. With thanks to The British Newspaper
Archive (www.BritishNewspaperArchive.co.uk).

James Spratt's remarkable love for dogs compelled him to seek a way to elevate the animal food industry. It was Spratt's belief that the "food makes the dog."[1] While at a boatyard in Liverpool, England, he observed stray dogs being thrown scraps and hard biscuits left over from the sailors' rations. These biscuits, known as hardtack,[2] were made of flour, salt, and water. They were briefly baked and then left to harden and dry in the outside air. In addition to salted meat and water, hardtack biscuits were the mainstay of a sailor's diet. Spratt was dismayed by the types of scraps stray dogs at the boatyards were eating; and he was inspired to create a new way to feed dogs. While others had previously made similar biscuit-type foods, James Spratt would be the first to revolutionize commercially prepared dog foods.

From the UK to the USA

Spratt was a successful inventor while in England during the mid to late 1800s. In 1861, his food received a patent and became known as the Meat Fibrine Dog Cake. The baked recipe consisted of rendered meat from local bison and vegetables such as beetroot. Local ads placed in the

Sportsman—such as the one below, dated Saturday, March 6, 1869—would frequently advertise the following:

> "JAMES SPRATT, Original Inventor and Patentee of pure Fibrine Dog Cakes. They contain 20 percent of pure fibrin, the dried unsalted gelatinous parts of prairie beef, ground wheat, iron, Sulphur and charcoal. The cakes are sweetened with that great antiscorbutic and luscious fruit, the date, that never clogs or creates thirst, and substitutes vegetable. This is the cheapest food requiring no cooking, will keep your dogs in condition without meat or other food the hair glossy, the dog regular, and as a sound diet obviates worms and distemper."

In 1876, approximately four years before Spratt's death, he received another registered trademark for his improvement in food for cattle (Figure 3). This special formula featured dates, which were used to quench animals' thirst and were suggested to supplement Spratt's Fibrine Meat Dog Cakes.

UNITED STATES PATENT OFFICE.

JAMES SPRATT, OF HORSTED KEYNES, ASSIGNOR TO EDWARD WYLAM, CHARLES JOHN WYLAM, AND GEORGE BEETHAM BATCHELOR, OF SURRY COUNTY, ENGLAND.

IMPROVEMENT IN FOOD FOR CATTLE.

Specification forming part of Letters Patent No. **180,953,** dated August 8, 1876; application filed May 16, 1876.

Figure 3: USPTO patent for improvement in food for cattle.

In this same year, a young man named Charles Cruft became an employee of Spratt and was quickly promoted to salesperson. Cruft—who in later years went on to organize the famous Crufts Dog Show in London—spent a great deal of time at dog shows, providing samples of the Meat Fibrine Dog Cake to competitors and attendees alike. Together, Spratt and Cruft set up booths and worked the dog show circuit to promote the original Meat Fibrine Dog Biscuit. Spratt's presence at these dog shows helped to form a long-lasting relationship between Spratt's Patent Ltd. and the American Kennel Club. Even after Spratt's death, the company continued to advertise their product on a regular basis in the *American Kennel Gazette*, often securing the coveted spot of magazine front cover (Figure 4).

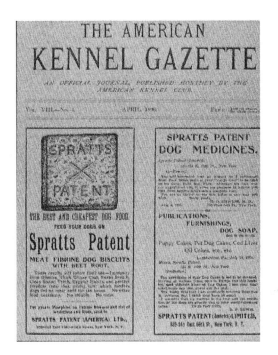

Figure 4: American Kennel
Gazette front cover 1889.

A few years before his death in 1878, Spratt sold his company to Edward Wylam, whom he'd met through Charles Cruft. In 1885, Spratt's Patent Ltd. expanded ownership rights to include CJ Wylam and Beetham Batcheor. These men invested two hundred thousand pounds between the three of them, and CJ became the director of the organization. The company went public in 1895. The goal was to take the company to America, Russia, and Canada.

By 1893, they had quite a lucrative business. Their balance sheet showed they had £90,000. According to the *Economist* (1894), a spokesperson for the Spratt company stated, "The Bermondsey factory is worked to nearly the extreme limit. Further capital is required for the natural expansion of the business to provide for necessary plant, machinery and to build an additional plant at Poplar" (Figure 5).

Figure 5: Spratt's Poplar Biscuit Factory.
Photo courtesy of Fabien Egot.

To put this in perspective, £90,000 in today's USD currency would be the equivalent of just over $42 million! This plant would eventually be recognized as the world's largest dog biscuit factory in the world. The men later opened a manufacturing plant in New York City and established the company at No. 18 Congress Street in Newark, New Jersey. According to *Doggy People* magazine (1902), even at this time in history, "individuals [gave] practically as good care to their own animals as to themselves and members of their own families."[3]

Spratt's Patent Ltd. was gaining recognition. In August 1886, the *Weekly Northwestern Miller* newspaper noted that "Spratt's Patent Limited may claim some share in the discovery [of the north pole], as Arctic explorers are now using them for their dogs. Spratt's having supplied the two most recent expeditions—those of Walter Wellman and Dr. Nansen."

Throughout the early 1900s, Spratt's company continued to support the American Kennel Club (AKC) through advertising on their magazine covers, which gave the small organization much needed capital. Spratt's company also displayed booths at AKC dog shows to promote their dog food (Figure 6).

OUR STAND AT THE FRANCO-BRITISH EXHIBITION. No. 139, COLONIAL AVENUE (NEAR INDIAN BUILDING).
ALSO IN ALIMENTATION BUILDING. No 4, STAND 65.
HEAD OFFICES: 24 & 25, FENCHURCH STREET, LONDON. E.C.

Figure 6: Photo circa 1908 of Spratt's exhibition booth in London.
All rights reserved. With thanks to the American
Kennel Club Archives Library.

Spratt's Patent Ltd. had the lion's share of the market for nearly five decades[4]—that is, until FH Bennett created a new product called Milk-Bone in 1908. For the first time in history, a dog biscuit became a regular item consumers purchased at the grocery store.

In 1922, the Chappel brothers of Rockford, Illinois, introduced Ken-L-Ration, the first canned dog food containing horse meat. When the Great Depression hit, most families were forced to shift their focus to conserving money and rationing food; so dog food became a luxury. Consumers cared more about cost than quality. During WWI, the Chappel brothers started out supplying horses to the United States government. After the war was over, they began to export horsemeat for use in dog food. Just about the time WWII arrived, canned dog food had 90 percent of the dog food market. Metal was a critical material at this time, as the government needed it to make aircraft and other machinery. Sales of canned food nearly halted because of this, but they regained a meager momentum after the war ceased. Slaughterhouses sold by-products and low-grade meat to dog food companies—which created a market for products that otherwise would have been discarded.

During the mid-1900s, Purina Dog Chow became the first dog food to be made with a new extrusion technology, which eventually became widely used by almost all pet food manufacturers. The extrusion process consisted of combining and cooking the ingredients together in a liquid form, then mechanically pushing the mixture through the extruder—thus expanding the kibble. These kibble pieces were lighter and larger, which gave the appearance of "getting more for your money." This kind of clever marketing in the dog food industry helped in the race to promote the product to the public.

General Mills bought Spratt's Patent Ltd. in 1950 for an undisclosed amount and continued to own and operate the company until 1961. At this time, Spillers—originally a flour milling company—acquired Spratt's for £3.94 million, and later changed the name to Spratt's Patent Holdings from Spratt's Patent Ltd. The name was changed again in 1972 to Spillers Food Limited.

Around the 1970s, a few celebrities begin to promote dog food on TV. Alpo made an ad featuring Lorne Greene, and Betty White promoted Science Diet. More celebrities appeared in television advertising and gained some momentum in new markets. Some of these companies added gravy-colored food dye to make the kibble appear more natural and pleasing to the consumer's eye. Pet advertisements emerged regularly in the media, as companies created new shapes and designs of pet food to be visually striking and tasty-looking. This strategy soon had pet food outpacing baby food sales. Aisles and shelf space were expanding enormously each year as more dog food companies joined the competition.

The next step for pet food companies was to produce "specialty diets" for specific diseases or disorders in more formulations. Dr. Mark Morris, DVM and founder of Hill's Pet Products, first came up with this notion, now called Science Diet. Following suit in this endeavor was Purina. Veterinarians championed these products, which were only available for purchase through a veterinary office. Companies such as Hill's soon started portraying dog food nutrition as "complex," and the public began to rely on their veterinarian's advice about pet nutrition. Veterinarians soon gained notoriety as nutrition experts with the advent of prescription pet food, which implied that certain food was more sophisticated.

In 1974, The National Research Council developed a protocol for nutritional values needed in pet food. That same year, the American Association of Feed Control Officials (AAFCO) was formed—the first group to help regulate pet food ingredients.

Former Spratt employee Chris Norman writes of his time working at Spratt's in 1972: "The company I worked for from 1972 was Spratt's Patent Ltd. . . . based in Cambridge Road, Barking, Essex. The company had been acquired by Spillers but was still being run as a separate company." This helps to show a major discovery the authors of this book made regarding Nutro's changes of ownership.

Chris goes on to say, "Spillers had their own pet food grocery division, but this was run as a competitor. The Spratt's product range still included a lot of the original favorites, including Cruckles, although from memory Bonio had been taken by Spillers. They also had a Petra range of products which were only available to the pet trade . . . to combat the problems of supermarkets crossing over into the pet food industry and . . . because of their buying power, undercutting smaller independents for like products. They also launched a 'big value' range of pet foods to compete at the lower end of the market, interestingly enough to compete with Spillers' budget range of 'bonus' dog food. I didn't understand this concept originally but began to realize that competition for shelf space was critical, and by running two companies side by side, you could gain double this shelf space."[5] Even four decades earlier, the concept of shelf space was being talked about and still is today.

The late 1900s saw "premium" dog foods as the newest trend in commercial pet food. Companies advertise their premium foods as being more nutritious for dogs, offering various blends for all stages of life—from puppy, maintenance, performance, to senior foods. Despite the "premium" labels, many of these companies were using old nutritional requirements from the 1970s. They could also sell these premium foods for a premium price, since consumers naturally considered the ingredients and formulations to be worth any extra expense. Some companies claimed to have superior ingredients, yet these same ingredients appeared on the labels of grocery-brand dog food.

Consumers nowadays have become more educated on nutrition—not only for themselves, but also for their pets. Many consumers began to read labels to sort out what the "premium" food *truly* was. Because companies need to include preservatives to extend the life of kibble, they began using chemicals like ethoxyquin, BHA, and BHT—which didn't sit well with many dog owners. Consumers rebelled and refused to buy from companies using these potentially cancer-causing ingredients,[6] along with products containing corn and by-products.

The new millennium brought even more changes in the industry. Over the end of the last decade, natural pet food became more critical to pet food labeling. Companies made official statements about being organic and containing human-grade ingredients. Today, consumers now want meat as the first ingredient; yet many companies are still producing food with upward of 50 percent grain, fillers, and grain by-products.

The infamous pet food recall of 2007 sent consumers into a frenzy over food safety and quality for their beloved dogs and cats. During this devastating incident, manufacturers unknowingly purchased wheat gluten tainted with melamine—a material widely used in plastics, adhesives, and dishware (*not* in pet food)—from a supplier in China. When the melamine was used in wheat gluten, it created a higher protein level content—thus making the wheat gluten appear to be a high-quality ingredient. The Food and Drug Administration (FDA) issued an alert on March 15, 2007, that certain foods were making pets sick and some were dying from the tainted food. One unnamed pet food manufacturer contacted the FDA to alert them to the fact that fourteen dogs and cats had perished while eating their food containing the suspected melamine. The death toll was far greater than this one report. Unfortunately, when pets began to consume the food, the results were fatal. All pet food manufacturers, including Nutro, felt the impact of this event; it hampered the company's bottom line as it approached the $700 million mark.

This incident, along with several other recalls, prompted consumers to become fearful about what they fed their pets. As a result, manufacturers went to great lengths to determine the origins of the ingredients they purchased. Many manufacturers began claiming their food was "made in the USA." Some even put American flags on bags of pet food to show an allegiance in purchasing ingredients or making the food in the US.

Dogs have gone from the barnyard, to the backyard, and finally to the bedroom. Small dog ownership is on the rise, and pets are now traveling companions with their parents. According to a 2016 Gallup poll, 76 percent of Americans have given their pet a present on Christmas; and 60 percent of pet owners believe owning a pet leads to a more satisfying lifestyle compared to non-owners.[7] We see people pushing their dogs in strollers, and pet-related clothing is trendy and fashionable. When the Great Recession hit in 2009–2010, the amount of money people spent eating out declined sharply; yet the purchases of pet food stayed constant.

Celebrity endorsements of pet-related items from people like Martha Stewart are becoming more prevalent. Former PetSmart CEO Bob Moran said, "The natural, organic trend is going to keep on getting bigger and bigger. We're also matching up with new vendors, new assortments, even proprietary brands . . . We have product partnerships with Martha Stewart, [Poison lead singer and reality-TV star] Bret Michaels, GNC, Marvel Comics, Toys 'R' Us. About 3 1/2 years ago, about 15% of product sales came from exclusive PetSmart products. Today, they're around 23%."[8]

Pets are woven into the fabric of our lives. With over 75 percent of American households owning a pet,[9] it is no wonder that the future of the pet industry has a very bright outlook.

CHAPTER 3: BUILDING THE EMPIRE

"If you work just for money, you'll never make it, but if you love what you're doing and you always put the customer first, success will be yours."

—Ray Kroc

According to two leading analysts at GfK (*Gesellschaft für Konsumforschung* [Society for Consumer Research])—the fourth largest market research organization in the world—global retail pet food sales have reached over a staggering $70 billion.[10] Of the $70 billion, North America comprises the largest spending continent, pulling in nearly 30 percent of the total alone. Table 1 shows us a comparison of total global revenue of baby food over the past nine years. Pet food for this same time frame was $59.3 billion in 2010 and $73.3 billion in 2015. Global pet food sales are significantly higher than baby food revenue.

Sales of Baby Food vs. Pet Food in Billions

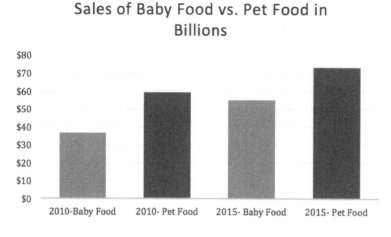

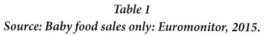

Table 1
Source: Baby food sales only: Euromonitor, 2015.

Over 131 million babies are born annually throughout the world[11]—each a potential consumer of baby food. Yet surprisingly, global sales of pet food have shot past baby food sales by *$15 billion*. A study conducted in 2012 by the American Veterinary Medical Association (AVMA) showed that more than 75 percent of US households own a dog or cat.[12] US households alone are responsible for owning more than 140 million dogs and cats, therefore making the pet food industry a powerhouse of consumer packaged goods.

So which companies are selling all this food? There are several usual suspects—such as Colgate-Palmolive (Hill's), Mars, and Nestle—but one major player, Procter & Gamble (P&G), is missing from the list these days. The world's top-ten pet food companies are represented in annual revenue as follows in Table 2.

COMPANY	COUNTRY	ANNUAL REVENUE
Mars Petcare, Inc.	USA	$17,224,400,000
Nestle Purina PetCare	USA	$11,917,000,000

Big Heart Pet Brands	USA	$2,280,300,000
Hill's Pet Nutrition	USA	$2,212,000,000
Diamond Pet Foods	USA	$1,150,00 0,000
Blue Buffalo	USA	$1,027,447,000
Spectrum Brands/ United Pet Group	USA	$800,000,000
Unicharm Corp.	JAPAN	$722,565,401
Deuerer	GERMANY	$721,100,000
Heristo AG	GERMANY	$700,000,000
TOTAL		*$38,754,812,401*

TABLE 2
Source: Pet food industry.

Out of the top-ten companies, Mars Petcare ascended with their 2014 P&G acquisition. Thanks to a $2.9 billion all-cash deal, Mars—a privately held company ranked fifth on the Forbes list of America's largest private companies—bought Procter & Gamble's pet food business. According to Reuters, the transaction handed over the reins of 80 percent of the US and select foreign countries' pet food business.[13]

Table 3 shows us the various brands these companies feature. You'll likely recognize some names, but many large private and publicly traded companies have been buying up smaller, independently owned pet food companies.

MANUFACTURER	BRANDS
Mars Petcare, Inc.	Nutro, Iams, Eukanuba, Greenies, California Natural, Innova, Pedigree, Little Whiskas, Cesar, Royal Canin
Nestle Purina PetCare	Alpo, Bakers, Beneful, Purina, Chef Michael's, Purina ONE, Friskies, Fancy Feast, Merrick, Felix, Castor & Pollux

Big Heart Pet Brands	Nature's Recipe, Milk-Bone, Kibbles 'n Bits, Gravy Train, Nine Lives, Meow Mix, Alley Cat,
Hill's Pet Nutrition	Science Diet
Diamond Pet Foods	Natural Balance, Diamond Naturals, CANIDAE, Chicken Soup, Country Value, Kirkland, Premium Edge, Professional, Solid Gold, Taste of the Wild
Blue Buffalo	BLUE Basics, BLUE Freedom, BLUE Wilderness, BLUE Life Protection Formula
Spectrum Brands/United Pet Group	None listed on website
Unicharm Corp.	Aiken Genki, Neko Genki, Gaines, Gin no Spoon, Gin no Sara
Deuerer	Private label manufacturer
Heristo AG	Saturn Petcare, Animonda Petcare

TABLE 3
Brands owned by manufacturers as of August 2016.

The first major shift in this trend was the sale of the Iams Company. Much like Nutro, Iams touted the fact that consumers could only find their products in pet specialty stores, not grocery or mass markets. Then in 1999, Iams owner Clay Mathile decided to sell his company to P&G. The owners of Nutro made a similar decision in May 2007, when Mars Incorporated purchased Nutro for over $2 billion. In Clay Mathile's book, *Dream No Little Dreams*, he refers to the top three premium pet food companies as Hills, Iams, and Nutro.[14]

You might have noticed that we refer to people with pets as "pet parents." They are not just dog or cat "owners"; consumers treat their canine and feline companions as members of the family. In fact, statistics tell us that two-thirds of pet owners would spend any amount—even go into debt—to save the life of their pet.[15] According to the American Pet

Products Association 2010–2011 Pet Survey, "over $11,000 will be spent on the lifetime of a [dog], even in times of a recession."[16] Consider these other statistics[17] on what pet owners think and do:

- 57 percent of pet owners surveyed would want a pet as their *only* companion if deserted on an island.
- 80 percent of survey respondents selected companionship as the major reason for having a pet.
- 72 percent of pet owners say that affection is their pets' most endearing trait.
- 79 percent of surveyed pet owners give their pets holiday or birthday presents.
- 33 percent of pet owners talk to their pets on the phone or through the answering machine.
- 62 percent of respondents often sign letters or cards from them and their pets.
- 55 percent of pet owners consider themselves as mom or dad to their pets.

Even decades before these results, the leadership at Nutro saw this wave of pet ownership becoming an increasingly integral part of Americans' daily lives. Nutro had been floating steadily out at sea for years, and the company was primed to finish building the empire when the 1990s rolled around. The organization was able to connect with consumers and create a powerful demand for their pet food—and they capitalized on this connection, along with the love affair people have with their pets.

CHAPTER 4: THE LINEAGE:
FROM MUSTANG TO MILKY WAY

"The quality of a person's life is in direct proportion to their commitment to excellence, regardless of their chosen field of endeavor."

—Vince Lombardi

John C. Saleen was born on April 6, 1918, in the small town of WaKeeney, Kansas, to a family who grew wheat and raised cattle on their family farm. John's grandfather, Olaf, had emigrated from Sweden with his parents before the turn of the century. John's parents decided to move the family west, and eventually settled in Redondo Beach, California. John was drafted into the Air Force in 1941 and served his country honorably during World War II (Figure 7). Upon his entry into the service, John had a strong desire to be a pilot. After all, he already had his pilot's license. Unfortunately, the colorblindness discovered during his physical entry examination prevented him from this endeavor. His youngest son, Mike, explains, "My dad was crushed to hear this."

Figure 7: Photo circa 1944.
Photo courtesy: Robyn Saleen.

Instead, John was assigned to be a crew member aboard B17 and B25 bombers as a radio operator, engineer, tail gunner, and Morse code reader. He was stationed in the Pacific Corridor, and he called Guam and the Philippines home for several years. Mike proudly yet humbly shared with me, "My dad was not the type of person to talk about his war service unless he was asked about it. He completed seventy-five missions fighting the Japanese—[and he] *volunteered* for the majority of these. His squadron was one of the lucky ones to survive the war and make it back home." Right after Japan surrendered, John's squadron flew their bomber home.

Steve, the eldest of John's three children, vividly recalls his father telling him of their return from Japan. As Steve was telling me this story, he sat back in his chair, folded his arms behind his head, and smiled as he shared, "My father was a tail gunner, and the crew decided they wanted to fly underneath the Golden Gate Bridge in San Francisco on their way returning to home base. They thought they might get in trouble—but hell, the war was over and they were happy to be alive. It was one last hurrah." John served honorably after arriving home as an instructor for B29s at March Air Reserve Base in Riverside, California.

During the time John was serving in the Air Force, his Uncle Herman started his own business, Pacific Dog Catering Company. This draft registration card (Figure 8) shows the relationship between Herman Saleen, his company (Pacific Dog Catering), and the photo shown in Figure 9.

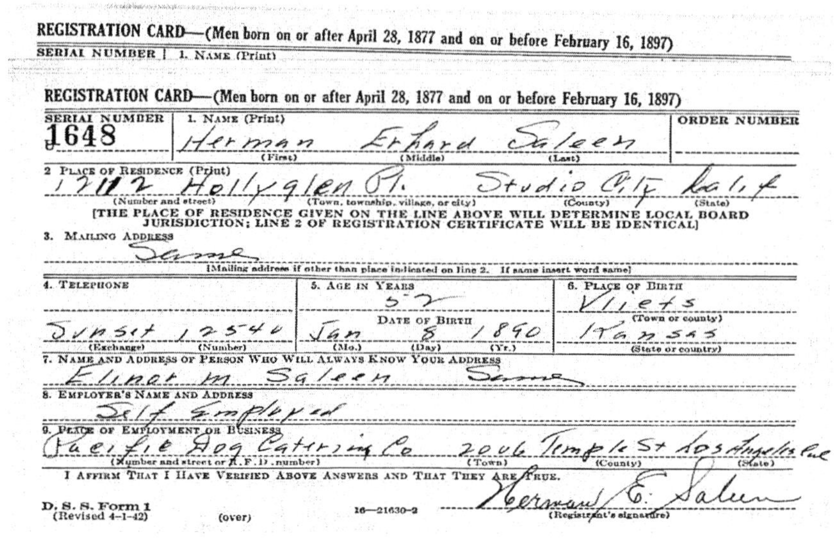

Figure 8: Herman Erhard Saleen's draft card.
Source: www.genealogy.com.

Herman left Wakeeny back in 1933 to start his new operation. Later, Albert—Herman's brother and John Saleen's father—sold the family farm and headed west to join his brother. Albert helped Herman with the fox farm business. Herman (Figure 9) taught his brother everything he knew about raising foxes and operating a farm. Herman also had a side business selling wet dog food. He owned his own slaughterhouse, which helped him in making the food.

Figure 9: Herman Erhard Saleen.
Source: www.genealogy.com.

Herman later developed a "meatloaf" type of fox food, which he determined would be excellent for dogs as well since it made their coats shiny and soft. Herman used to sell the meatloaf to a variety of customers and made these deliveries in his company vehicle (Figure 10). Herman eventually sold his wet food to Kal Kan.

Figure 10: Herman Erhard Saleen's delivery vehicle.
Resourced from www.genealogy.com.

After John was honorably discharged from the Air Force, he decided to remain in Southern California to live near his parents. He joined a youth organization at the local church called Luther League. During a function one evening, John met a beautiful young woman named Evelyn. They were married on October 13, 1945, lived in Whittier, and were founding members of a local Lutheran church whose congregation they belonged to for the next fifty years. John and Evelyn's daughter, Robyn, lovingly recalls, "Dad was an avid reader and loved Western novels, reading poetry, and watching golf and auto racing. People looked to my dad as an example of how to live an honest life, and he took very good care of other people. He was the everyman's man."

While John held several jobs after the military, none of the positions seemed to provide anything he was passionate about. It wasn't too long before his Uncle Herman asked him if he would like to manage his delivery route for Pacific Dog Catering for a few weeks while he went out of town. During this time, John found his purpose. He quickly became an advocate for animals and had a yearning for pet nutrition. John and his Uncle Herman became business partners in the Pacific Dog Food Catering Company (Figure 11).

Figure 11: Storefront of Pacific Dog Catering and Nutro Dog Food.
Photo credit: Mike and Desi Saleen.

Mike Saleen says, "I think it must have been my Uncle Herman that owned Nutro Dog Food. We don't have any documents and I was not even born yet. My wife, Desi, recalls my mom telling us that she and my dad bought a small house in October 1945 for the purpose of [what we'd now call] 'flipping' it. The $5,000 they made on the house became the down payment for the business my father wanted to buy from Uncle Herman. The house was sold in April 1947." While reviewing old documents with Steve Saleen, we can see business transactions regarding Nutro equipment that validate what Mike recalls.

According to the USPTO (United States Patent and Trademark Office), John Saleen renewed the Nutro Dog Food Company trademark in 1952 from the family of Herben Serois. Serois had started the company in 1931, and received approval to use the trademark Nutro in 1936.

Little has been recorded on Herben Serois (Figure 12) and his ownership of the Nutro Dog Food Company. We know that he was born on July 31, 1879, in Kankakee, Illinois, to parents Anthony Serois and Josephine Levegue. They had two sons; Edwin, born in 1884, and Herben. According to Herben's World War II draft card, we can see that he had brown hair, brown eyes, and was five feet six inches tall. We have been unable to locate any other photos of Herben or his family. Herben appears to have been married twice: first to Dalia, with whom he had two sons—Clyde and Byron—and later to Vivian, who was twelve years his junior. Vivian was fifty when Herben passed away on October 2, 1942. They had no children, although Vivian had a son, Curtis.

Herben Serois

Funeral services for Herben Serois, 63 a dog food manufacturer, who died Friday at his home, 2617 Waverly Drive, will be conducted at 2 30 p m tomorrow at the Wee Kirk o' the Heather Interment will be in Forest Lawn Memorial Park Serois leaves his widow, Mrs Vivian Serois, a brother, Edwin Serois, St. Anne, Ill, and three sisters, Mrs Lilly Denno, Monett, Mo, Mrs Flossy Beisz Peotone, Ill, and Mrs Aurora Adams, Toledo, O

Figure 12: Herben Serois's obituary.
Source: www.genealogy.com,
Los Angeles Times, **October 4, 1942.**

Based on limited newspaper articles, Herben appears to have been fairly active in the pet industry. The *Hollywood Citizen News* included in a 1936 article that "Dog lovers [proclaimed] the Ventura County Dog Fanciers' Association first annual show . . . as one of the most successful shows ever presented in Southern California . . . The show was one of the best ever . . . according to H. Serois, manufacturer of a nationally known dog food, who attends all the dog shows."

Later, John Saleen went on to purchase other small, pet-care related companies such as Barnett, Mackall's, and Krill. Eventually, these all rolled up into the Nutro Dog Food Company. In 1963, seeking to add to his company, John sent a letter to Spratt's requesting permission to use their name and their response is shown in Figure 13. This letter would have been the first contact John Saleen made with Spratt's. There was no other documentation found to gauge the final response from the English company. John never sold Spratt's in the US.

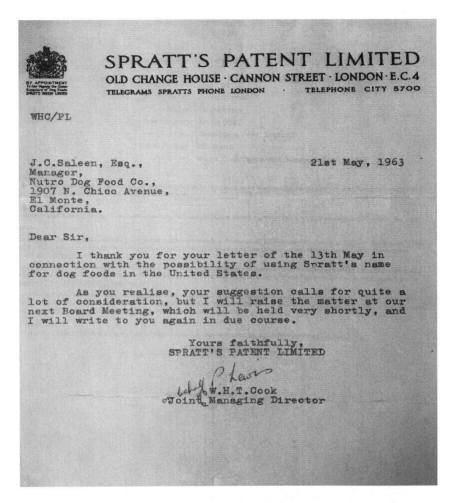

Figure 13: Response letter to John Saleen.
Document courtesy of The Saleen Family.

Though John Saleen had no formal college education, he was a self-taught chemist with a knack for formulating dog food. John was the one to formulate the pet food and other Nutro supplements the company produced. Natural nutrition was a critical component in making these products, and John was considered a pioneer in creating health foods for pets. His active involvement in the pet industry compelled him to attend pet trade shows regularly. One particular trade show proved to be a pivotal moment in John's life.

Ed Brown, a sales representative for Lee Mar (a distributor of pet-related hard goods) was attending a local pet industry convention back in 1973 when he strategically placed himself at a lunch table next to John Saleen. The two men had a conversation that lasted the entire meal, as Ed inquired as to why he should feed his dog Nutro. John spoke of the all-natural ingredients and the lustrous skin and coat Ed should expect to see within a few weeks of feeding Nutro to his dog. Ed was so mesmerized by the passion that John showed about his product and his company that he wondered what it would be like to own Nutro.

The ensuing years led to occasional conversations between the two solopreneurs. Ed continued to ponder how he could raise enough capital to buy the company *and* persuade John to sell it to him. Ed consistently reminded John that members of his family did not have a strong enough interest to keep the company going with John's same passion—but Ed did. John Saleen had struggled to get at least one of this three grown children to take over the family business.

John's health began to fail as he got older, and his children still showed no interest in operating Nutro Products. In 1975, John decided to have one last conversation with his three grown children about running the business after he retired. His middle child, Mike, was intrigued by the law; and he would go on to graduate from Whittier College and attend Loyola to earn his law degree. Robyn, the youngest of the kids, ran a pet store; and the oldest son, Steve, was interested in racing cars. Of John's three children, Steve Saleen had spent the most time in the family business. Steve and his younger brother spent summers and days off from school working for their father, and they both speak fondly and remember well the days when they would drive to one of three bread stores in the area. Steve revealed, "My father would drive me and my brother to Langendorf, Helm, or Weber's Bread to purchase wheat bread to use as an ingredient in our products. My dad would drive the Ford station wagon along with a wooden flatbed with metal siding to pick up the bread weekly. Once we got back to the plant, me and my brother would unload the bread [Figure 14]. Yeah, we'd play around a bit and we would jump from the roof of the station wagon and land onto the pillows of Wonder Bread beneath us. What fun days!" Mike emphasized, "Our dad analyzed the dog food we made and wanted to make sure we were making and selling health food for dogs. In doing his research, he found that Langendorf Bakery used a superior [brand of] flour as an ingredient—and that's why we used their bread in our early formulation."

Figure 14: Nutro Dog Food Company building.
Photo courtesy of Steve Saleen.

Steve eventually decided to attend USC and major in business, then graduated in 1971. As Steve grew up, he found himself participating more and more in the family business he'd come to know so well. He helped in making the food, conducting deliveries, and after graduating college, was assigned to be a temporary salesman for Vern—an employee who had suffered a heart attack and could not work. Temporary soon turned into permanent, and for the next several years, Steve set out to make his mark in the pet industry.

Steve quickly discovered that many pet food retailers did not have good marketing tactics. Regional malls were being developed at this time, and many of these malls had pet stores. So Steve decided to go back to school and take some post-graduate classes. In one of his courses—which taught students how to lay out stores and create merchandising plans—Steve recalls, "I remember I was sitting next to the president of Ralph's supermarket!" Steve admired the fact that a person of the president's stature was present.

Steve combined the merchandising schematics he learned with his own ideas and created planograms to make the most of the pet shops to whom Nutro was selling. He was instrumental in developing these initial formal marketing ideas for Nutro as they began to control more of the retailers' growth. Steve recalls, "I was single at the time, and therefore able to dedicate much time to helping the retailers in Southern California grow their business. We would take small unorganized stores, plan out their shelving, and create a beautiful, well organized store that made sense to the shopper." Steve further shares, "I realized it felt like I was working 24/7 and often late—nine, ten, eleven o'clock at night. We were controlling a lot of what the store was doing, and our business was really flourishing." During this time in the mid-1970s, Nutro's business was not just manufacturing; it also included distributing hard goods for pets, such as flea control products, fish supplies, and many others.

Steve had other impacts on his father's dog food manufacturing business, including collaborating on the creation of the Nutro logo. (This occurred shortly after his father sold Nutro.) The Saleens also owned retail pet and feed stores that Steve helped to set up, the first of which was Pet Barn in Sacramento, California. Since Steve was the eldest of the three

Saleen kids, John leaned on him quite a bit to help run many of the day-to-day operations.

As he found his compass and his true north in life, Steve became very passionate about cars, racing, *and* his soon-to-be wife. As Steve reflected, he admitted, "Between dog food and cars, cars were my first love." For years, he went back and forth between racing and dog food. His passion for pet food eventually waned, while his passion for cars steadily rose. Steve found he was truly at his best when racing cars. Eventually, he had the opportunity—as well as his wife's blessing and support—to make his mark in the automotive industry. In 1983, Steve founded Saleen Autosport.

John Saleen eventually realized his children did not have the same calling to continue with Nutro that he had. When he struck out with all three, John called Ed Brown and said, "Put a price on it and let's chat."

CHAPTER 5: A LEAP OF FAITH

"Faith is to believe what you do not yet see; the reward
for this faith is to see what you believe."

—St. Augustine

In 1975, the average cost of a home was $43,400,[18] and the average American's income was barely topping $16,000. A postage stamp was a dime, a loaf of bread cost a quarter, and a tank of gas for the average car was less than ten dollars. So when Ed Brown went home and asked his wife, "Honey, we can build an incredible future we have always wanted for $300K . . . What do you think?" her reply was one of support—yet she gently encouraged her husband that it might be in their best interest to find a business partner.

Ed was born on February 23, 1927, in Duluth, Minnesota. He met his wife, Geraldine, on a blind date when they were sixteen years old. Six years later, they married when Ed was a senior at the University of Minnesota, majoring in business and economics. Before asking Geraldine's father for her hand in marriage, he devised a plan to save up one thousand dollars for their honeymoon. After saving the money, Ed mentioned to Geri's father that he was a very rich man and asked for her hand in marriage. Ed fondly recalls, "I fell madly in love with her. She was the cutest thing in the world." As of 2016, they have been married seventy-three years. Ed confessed, "I love her more and more every day, and I don't know where it keeps coming from."

One reason is likely her wisdom and insight, since Geri provided some good advice that day in 1975. Ed agreed with his wife, then called up a dear friend of his named Don Taffy to discuss this business opportunity. Ed said to Don, who worked with a professional management group, "I am looking for a person with the right stuff to help build a pet food empire." Don made several phone calls and had someone in mind with whom he thought Ed should collaborate.

Sometimes when two ingredients come together, the partnership they form is immensely successful. Consider how the truly revolutionary combination of peanut butter and chocolate made the world-famous Reese's Peanut Butter Cup. This is precisely what happened when Ed Brown and David Traitel decided to join forces. They were two ingredients that— once combined—forever changed the pet industry.

And so began this very successful partnership. Some people wondered how two such driven individuals could manage the business and not let egos get in the way, but the answer was simple, really; they each took charge of the area that suited their strengths. Ed was the relationship builder, who easily created a market by asking one simple question: "So tell me, Tiger, does your dog have hot spots or dry, itchy skin?" Ed truly had a gift for making his customer feel as if they were the most important—and *only*—person in the world. He didn't have to work hard at being heartfelt and genuine; he exuded authenticity and honesty everywhere he went.

David was the visionary. According to one past CEO, "David had an uncanny ability to see into the future, much like a Steve Jobs." Another marketing manager emphasized, "Dave's level of integrity, honesty, financial acumen, and ability to be a wholesome and genuine individual made him the ideal leader for managing the financial and strategic aspects of the company." Dave himself once shared, "Great companies are seldom constructed around any particular product. They are instead enrobed by a design. A product has a finite lifetime due to the competitive forces of the marketplace. Conversely, a properly conceived corporate design contains within its nucleus a self-regeneration potential. This enables an organization to transcend the vagaries of product-based competition."

It is this "design"—which includes the company's strategy and culture—that interests us as authors most. Qualitative surveys—distributed to many associated with the Nutro business who were hired before 2007—have explored issues around this design, and we've conducted a great many personal interviews with stakeholders. Feedback from survey participants are sprinkled throughout this book. We have intentionally left most names of individuals out, especially after reading one person's response to the question: *Who inspired you the most while working at Nutro?* The heartfelt response was, "It wasn't so much the individuals as the Nutro spirit that inspired [me]. No one was indispensable and time and time again we saw where individuals came and left, but the spirit continued."

Our survey respondents' departmental affiliations are shown below. It is heavily skewed toward sales, as that department did have the largest number of employees working in it. The marketing department had the next highest number of respondents and employees.

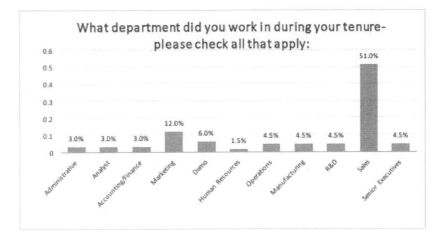

Figure 15
Distribution of survey respondents' departments

CHAPTER 6: TREES DON'T GROW TO THE SKY

"Whoever sows sparingly will also reap sparingly, and who-
ever sows generously will reap generously."

—2 Corinthians 9:6

In the early years, Nutro consistently saw growth in the 30–40 percent range—which was quite impressive for such a young company. Knowing that this type of growth could not be sustained over a long period, Dave Traitel used to say, "Trees don't grow to the sky." In other words, he knew it might be time to recalculate the growth they were expecting and the goals they were setting for the company—since 40 percent might be a bit *too* high to continue. While Dave certainly wanted his company to do well, he also knew the importance of being realistic. The strategies that grew from the design of the company stem from what the organization has repeatedly called "belly-to-belly" selling: being in front of people who need to be educated on the product and understand the benefits to using Nutro.

Nutro employed four main "belly-to-belly" strategies up until mid-2000. According to one past president of the company, "There was no need to be first." Those with a competitive nature might wonder why; but the short- and long-term goal was simple: "Sell one bag at a time." This might seem like a rather slow way to ramp up and conduct business and gain market share and sales, and Nutro didn't share any lengthy company blueprints or five-year plans. Their tactic was to employ straightforward sales strategies, thereby allowing the company to nimbly outmaneuver the competition—an approach that ultimately proved incredibly successful.

These four major strategies—shown in Figure 16—were the center of the organization. Its members unanimously agreed to: 1. Sell on the differential; 2. Sell by conversion; 3. Gain recommendation; and 4. Sell belly-to-belly using the best people.

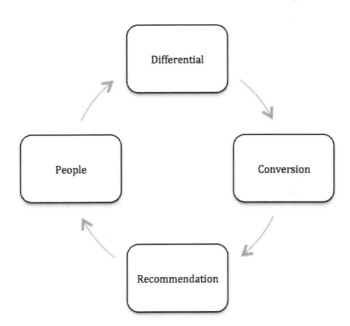

Figure 16: Belly-to-belly strategies of Nutro.

These might not be glamorous strategic titles, but they allowed a company to go from zero to $800 million in two decades—*without* the financial assistance of banks or venture capitalists. Each element of this approach played an integral part in Nutro's success.

CHAPTER 7: BELLY-TO-BELLY STRATEGY #1: DIFFERENTIAL

"Success is not measured by what you do compared to what others do. It is measured by what you do with the ability God gave you."

—Zig Ziglar

American academic Michael Porter—known for his theories on business strategies—has said, "A company can outperform rivals only if it can establish a difference it can preserve." The difference for Nutro was twofold: the product's ingredients, and the fact that it was only sold in pet specialty outlets—not supermarkets. This distinction was expressed fondly through the slogan "The Difference Is Nutrition"—the message Nutro used to go to market. It did not matter if it was an employee in accounting, sales, manufacturing, marketing, or elsewhere; every member of the company was passionately selling the product. It was common for Nutro team members to "convert" consumers in a variety of places—on airplanes, in line at the grocery store, and of course, in conversations with friends and family.

The ingredient differential was something that most of the "big guys"—competitors like Hill's and Procter & Gamble—were not using. In fact, they were working arduously to go to market and battle with their "me too" ingredients. Nutro first used the differential strategy in the mid-1950s, under previous owner John Saleen. John's love of nutrition and chemistry allowed him to create Nutro's all-natural products. Nutro later hired a young, bright, and headstrong nutritional authority named Dr. Sharon Machlik, who joined the company to create a new line of cat food. Instead, Dr. Machlik began to enhance a product line called Max, which launched in 1980 and contributed significantly to the company's early success. Max's ingredients—or rather, lack thereof—became the company mantra for decades: "No heads, no feet, no guts."

The big guys *were* selling heads, feet, and guts in their ingredient decks—so Nutro began to use this ingredient differential in all recipes moving forward. Dr. Machlik was passionate about the research, the equipment, and the process. She created a proprietary blend of ingredients that the company was able to use fifteen years before anyone else had even considered taking a similar approach, truly putting Nutro ahead of the pack.

The difference allowed Nutro to bring superior value to the consumer, which made Nutro's competitors easy prey to sell against. Nutro used chicken meal instead of poultry by-products, rice instead of ground yellow corn, and sunflower oil rather than animal fat. The company could sell these premium ingredients at a premium price in comparison to the substitute ingredients that the competition offered. Consumers could feed less of the product to their pets since it was more digestible; and the fat source created a shinier skin and coat, which meant less shedding. This unique combination was Nutro's main selling strategy. Of the recipes created after Max, the foremost impact was Natural Choice Lamb and Rice. In fact, most executives at Nutro would agree that in 1991 the creation of Natural Choice Lamb and Rice was the tipping point for the company.

The company was able to continue their differential tactic by making power claims about the product's performance. Statements like "Guaranteed to Improve Skin & Coat" made the product "bulletproof"—a term Nutro employees commonly used to indicate the product was reliable and impervious to failure.

The success of Max made way for other formula creations at Nutro. The creations that followed Natural Choice were *all* assembled by Dr. Gary Crosslin, a quiet man with a brilliant mind. Just like Dr. Sharon Machlik, Dr. Crosslin had an enormous blend of talents. He knew the intricacies of how ingredients would behave in the extruders, as well as each ingredient's digestibility and palatability. After receiving test results from vice president of technical services—Rudy Leschke and his team of technical advisors— Drs. Crosslin and Machlik knew precisely what to change in the formula to enhance performance, palatability, and digestibility every time. The entire research and development team worked tirelessly on implementing and perfecting processes that improved the products, making them even *more* bulletproof.

These power claims allowed retailers to sell the product successfully as well. Pet food sales were coming primarily from grocery and mass markets back in the late '70s, but the second fold of the differential strategy dictated that Nutro only be available in pet specialty stores. This meant that Nutro needed to change not only the brand a consumer was shopping for, but also a consumer's shopping *patterns*. Asking a pet owner to buy Nutro would require them to make an additional stop to pick up Fido's food—and that was where the next strategy came in.

CHAPTER 8: BELLY-TO-BELLY STRATEGY #2: CONVERSION

"If you can't feed a hundred people, then feed just one."

—Mother Teresa

Selling by conversion—also known as "selling one bag at a time"—was the second strategy Nutro employed. It was a very simplistic and rather modest approach compared to brands like P&G, Colgate Palmolive, and other large consumer packaged goods companies who used media such as TV as their main mode of marketing. Selling one bag at a time was like taking the long way—or "The Road Less Traveled." This meant that Nutro employees would have a conversation with one individual, during which they passionately shared all the benefits of feeding the product to their pets. It was a conversation that Nutro's people—and not just the sales team—used to genuinely connect and learn about someone's dog or cat, educate people on ingredients, and make a product recommendation to improve the life of that pet.

To be able to convert a customer was a badge of honor within the company. The competitive environment encouraged the salespeople in particular to convert five people a day—a goal that was later changed to seven people a day. Salespeople interacted with everyone in the pet and feed stores, including the consumers themselves.

Converting seven people a day might not seem *that* impactful. In the beginning, when the company employed just five salespeople, it was slow going. So they decided that for every ten new trucks of pet food sold, they'd hire a new salesperson. "Sell more, hire more" soon became a tactic the team used to ramp up sales. Just ten short years later, the sales team had gone from 5 people to 125—and in another 10, the team nearly topped 350 people.

The reason was again simple: Sell the food on the store shelf to the consumer; the retailer then needs to reorder; the distributor has to reorder to fill their *own* pipeline; and sales generate exponentially. In 1976, there was one remarkable salesperson—Ed Brown. Some people imagine the typical salesperson as the fast-talking, dishonest, used-car seller, whose primary aim is to get the sale—not help the customer get what they need. Ed could not have been more different from this stereotype. He had an uncanny ability to remember a store owner's name, along with all their employees' names and pertinent information about what was going on in their lives. Ed made people feel as if they were of the utmost importance. He could make a connection with anyone, and before long, he was preaching the gospel of chicken, rice, and lamb.

Ed believed in the power of conversion—which was a critical outlook as the one and only salesperson in 1976. He drove around the West Coast in his Celebrity station wagon, traveling from San Diego, up through Los Angeles, and into San Francisco, where he sold store owners on the importance of stocking Nutro in their stores. Twenty-five years later, one salesperson explained it this way: "Conversion was the strategy, but it unfolded in an amazing way. Committing to [converting] five people per day to Nutro . . . forced us to be in the stores telling the story—and we were good at what we did. The interesting side effect was that we were there to capture every opportunity and tied up so much of the retailer's money into our displays and expansions that it left them with little left to put behind other brands. They had to sell *us* to make room for the next display . . . but, guess who was there selling the next display? We were. Conversion became floor space, shelf space, and retail domination. You can't sell competitive product if you don't have the money to buy it, or space to sell it."

With more true conversions, consumers readily bought the product and became loyal customers who would then tell others about Nutro. Once a consumer with an itchy, scratchy dog saw a glossier skin and coat and a happier, more comfortable pet after feeding her Nutro, she became a customer for the life of that pet. This became the power of conversion, which translated into "gaining recommendation."

CHAPTER 9: BELLY-TO-BELLY STRATEGY #3: RECOMMENDATION IS KING

"People often say that motivation doesn't last. Well, neither does bathing—that's why we recommend it daily."

—Zig Ziglar

Gaining recommendation was a daily if not by-the-minute ritual that involved several steps. First, it meant having a conversation that involved a variety of questions, normally starting with "Do you have a dog or a cat?" and followed with "What is your dog's name?" The conversation continued to engage the pet parent until the salesperson could make a recommendation. Loyal consumers who fed the product to their pets and told others about their positive experience added to this recommendation process— thereby selling additional pet owners on the concept and food. Having "recommenders" helped increase sales. Recommendations also came from the store staff, when consumers asked, "What food should I feed my dog or cat?" or "What food do you use?" The desired response was Nutro.

Retailers had great reasons to recommend the food. Often, store employees were rewarded or thanked for these efforts and received free food from Nutro for their own animals. Back in the 1980s, the average federal minimum wage for a retail employee was $3.35[19]—and a forty-pound bag of Nutro Natural Choice was $24.99. It would therefore take an hourly employee nearly eight hours or one full workday to pay for a bag that size. The company realized this discrepancy and wanted to thank those recommenders with a free bag of food, in hopes that the recommender would continue to advocate Nutro to new consumers.

On the last day of one national sales meeting, the character known as "Father Dewey" conducted his first appearance—or, rather skit—based on the importance of gaining recommendation. Father Dewey was playfully dressed in a black dress shirt with a white tab collar commonly used by clergy. He proceeded to give his first "sermon" on the gospel of chicken, rice, and lamb, which became known as the 10 Nutro Consumer Commandments (Appendix A). The room filled with roaring laughter—and probably a bit of bewilderment from some who were taken aback by the skit's religious theme. However, everyone stood as we all recited the 10 Consumer Commandments, which further showed the allegiance we had the retailer's best interest. We were all then served a small thimble-size cup of apple juice to toast our commitment to the 10 Consumer Commandments.

Recommendation helped all salespeople in the organization increase their sales. An employee who had a "Nutro store"—meaning that everyone in the store was a Nutro recommender—secured some serious bragging rights. These stores were worth their weight in gold; they were highly valued and contributed to the company's overall success. These Nutro stores offered fast and continued growth and were truly the keys to the kingdom of Nutro's success. Even the competition knew it. Salespeople considered any attempt by a competitor to "take" one of these stores to be a personal affront, and the competitor could expect to feel the heat come back tenfold.

CHAPTER 10: BELLY-TO-BELLY
STRATEGY #4: PEOPLE

"If you want one year of prosperity, grow grain. If you
want ten years of prosperity, grow trees. If you want
one hundred years of prosperity, grow people."

—Chinese Proverb

People were the conduit to all things at Nutro. Every piece of information traveled by and through people, no matter what team you worked on. Nutro made a conscious choice to use the word *team*, rather than *department*, to illustrate the connectedness of Nutro's people and emphasize how they worked so seamlessly together. In his book *Good to Great*, author Jim Collins discusses having the "right people in the right seat on the bus." While I have always loved this quote and refer to it frequently, I came upon an article Collins wrote called "Hitting the Wall: Realizing that Vertical Limits Aren't."[20] In it, Collins refers to an article written by James Logan called "Mount Robson's Emperor Face," in which Logan recounts his third attempt and successful 1978 summit on the legendary Emperor Face Mountain with his climbing partner, Mugs Stump.[21] Together, Logan and

Stump decided that they would climb the highest peak in the Canadian Rockies—a summit topping 12,994 feet. Collins makes the point when telling this story that it is not the *what* of the strategy that is important; it's *who* you are doing it with. The person James Logan took with him to face this challenge is what helped him reach the top.

Dave Traitel and Ed Brown scaled the mountain of pet food together. Each brought a set of strengths to the organization, and capitalized on those strengths. As discussed previously, people have described Dave as a visionary with excellent business acumen, much like Steve Jobs. Those around him saw Dave as a genuine leader, a man of the utmost honesty and integrity. He was a truth-seeker, someone who knew the company's numbers extremely well and had the gut instincts to make the right financial decisions. Despite this intuition, Dave always sought others' opinions and always remained open to hearing other sides when debating an issue. He took risks, willing to go the distance and play ball against "the big guys"— and he *won*, time and time again. Together, Dave and Ed demonstrated the importance of deciding "Who are we going to do this with?" when undertaking a significant endeavor. They employed a team of amazing people over the years, all of whom are noted in this book's Dedication.

As this once-small Southern California company headed north, east, and internationally, it grew its human capital into the best team in the pet food industry. To enjoy this kind of success, Nutro's people spanned a variety of roles and functions—and all played essential parts in building this remarkable organization.

Sales and Marketing

Some organizations are marketing organizations supported by sales. However, Nutro was just the opposite—and everyone knew it. It was a sales-driven company supported by marketing. What the salespeople wanted, the salespeople got; and the people in these two roles worked hand in hand. As the company grew, salespeople who did well were promoted to sales managers; then sales managers who did well were promoted to marketing. The sales team communicated frequently and passionately what they were hearing and seeing out in the field to the marketing team. In turn, the marketing team worked relentlessly and passionately to create programs, promotions, and products—in record time. In fact, they completed many product introductions within ninety days—going from inception to design, formulation, marketing, packaging, and manufacturing in just three months. According to some marketing gurus, this process can often take anywhere from eighteen months to years—sometimes even longer. The interconnectedness of Nutro's team is what allowed employees to use the free flow of information to seal their quick, competitive advantage.

Executive Level

The company's executive leadership saw the big picture and created a vision for the future. A decade before owner Dave Traitel sold the company, he allowed the then-president to begin interviewing other future presidents. He knew that Nutro needed a succession plan. If *you* ran an independently owned and operated family business—and no one in the family wanted to operate that business in coming years—what would *you* do? Odds are that you would sell it. So the vision was to hire a new co-president who would slowly integrate into the organization, take the helm, and financially prepare it for its eventual sale. This plan took nearly ten years to finalize.

Dave frequently reminded people at Nutro's national sales meetings that there were always some offers on the table to purchase the company. During one period in the late 1990s, rumors were running rampant about a possible purchase. Dave announced at a sales meeting, "Yes, some of you may have heard we were approached, and as of right now, we are not selling to Mars—the company or the planet." Dave was proud to be Nutro's sole proprietor.

Distributors

The strategy of putting people first went beyond the boundary of Nutro's employees. Nutro sought to partner with individuals and organizations they perceived to be the best distributors. One might assume this meant that distributors received the utmost respect, kindness, and care; unfortunately, this was not the always the case. Often, both parties experienced a Nutro-distributor partnership that was somewhat adversarial. The company viewed some distributors as a credit and delivery mechanism for the product, and as a result, some felt used and abused at the close of every month. One general manager of a distributor describes his experience this way: "[Nutro was] holding our distributorship over our heads. We were threatened with the possibility of not being a Nutro distributor if we did not make our monthly number. And it felt like a regular occurrence." Yet if you asked these very same distributors who were the hardest-working, most dedicated sales team, they would tell you team Nutro—every time. Certainly no company is perfect, and how Nutro treated their distributors was certainly a shortcoming. It was a love-hate relationship at times.

The "With Whom" Connection

Everyone in the organization was passionate about the product they sold. Each person truly believed that Nutro was bulletproof. If someone did not hold this belief, he or she likely didn't work at Nutro for long. The company was a family that spanned fifty states and over twenty-six countries, and the product sold on six of the seven continents. We greeted each other warmly with a hug at meetings. The company was small enough for all employees to know each other well. As one team member fondly remembers, "We shared stories about successes at work and celebrated successes at home and with our families. I knew every one of my coworkers' families from their spouses to their kids. We grew more to love each other in friendship than simply . . . as coworker[s]. This is [especially] interesting, because I never had a coworker who lived less than 120 miles from me.

[But] distance was no issue . . . we lived with one another, fought with one another, and loved one another."

One colleague suggested that the law of attraction was at play at Nutro—that is, that people simply attract whatever they think about, positive or negative. Most folks at Nutro were like-minded and constantly heard that they were absolutely the best in the business. In fact, "The World's Best Pet Food" was a phrase that people adopted when telling the Nutro Story and converting a new consumer. Each person lived and breathed this mantra with every fiber in their being—and as one team member explains, "It was the people who made the company so worthwhile. So many dedicated workers. We all believed in the product and the philosophy."

The following excerpt comes from the poem, "What Will Matter," written by Michael Josephson in 2003, is an example of not "what we had to do, yet rather, what we gave" to each other:

> Ready or not, some day it will all come to an end.
> There will be no more sunrises, no minutes, hours or days.
> All the things you collected, whether treasured or forgotten
> will pass to someone else…
> It won't matter whether you were beautiful or brilliant…
> So what will matter?
> How will the value of your days be measured?
> What will matter is not what you bought
> but what you built, not what you got but what you gave…
> What will matter is not your competence
> but your character…
> What will matter is how long you will be remembered,
> by whom and for what…
> Choose to live a life that matters.

Working in this organization certainly did consume a lot of time; yet people generously gave their time to a cause they believed in. Therefore, it did not seem like work for many employees. As one past employee recounts, "Working at Nutro didn't feel like a job; the relationships that were created will never be forgotten."

One past president emphasized, "It is equally important to note that the *consistency* of the strategy was a strategy as well." Any team who practices their plays over and over again will improve and excel. Vince Lombardi, whom many consider the world's best football coach in history, said to his teams: "The difference between a successful person and others is not a lack of strength, not a lack of knowledge, but rather in a lack of will." Nutro's belief in and execution on these four key attributes showed that consistency and perseverance can take a company very far.

CHAPTER 11: CREATING CAMELOT: THE NUTRO CULTURE

"Customers will never love a company until the employees love it first."

—Simon Sinek

We've all heard the question: "What came first: the chicken or the egg?" The Nutro equivalent of this question was: "Which came first: the product or the people?" We know it was the company founders' intention to create a corporate design that contains a "self-regeneration potential"—so we believe that the people came first. Nutro's employees served as the nucleus of the organization. These team members were central to the creation of everything, and the senior leadership team—as the ones who helped to shape the company—knew it better than anyone.

People who worked at Nutro went so far as to describe the culture and the way that all team members felt—about both the company and each other—as "Camelot." Some people may not be familiar with the legend of Camelot, a mystical city representing a magical place in time, where all members of its community share the same passion and purpose. Camelot is a place where people come together to celebrate goodness, and where the impossible is made possible. It's the perfect blend of harmony and good-will, and you know when you have been there because you have felt this experience firsthand.

There are a few other words that we feel describe the uniqueness of Nutro's culture. *Mojo* is one, defined by Merriam-Webster as "a power that may seem magical and that allows someone to be very effective, successful, etc." Mojo is the power to get things done. The following description from Marshall Goldsmith is spot-on: "Mojo is the moment when we do some-thing that's purposeful, powerful, and positive and the rest of the world recognizes it."[22]

So what is *it*? Mihaly Csikszentmihalyi, a Hungarian psychologist calls it *flow*: the "effortless action [people] feel in moments that stand out as the best in their lives."[23] For us, *it* is the culture that Nutro created that produced a competitive advantage and enabled people within the organi-zation to move mountains. As demand increased, the little giant moved eastward to serve more consumers. To say the culture simply used positive psychology to capitalize on the human spirit and bring creativity, intrinsic motivation, and optimism to life does not fully explain Nutro's mojo. It was more than that.

According to Schein, a Harvard Ph.D. culture is based on three prin-ciples; (a) artifacts, or observable actions within a group, (b) understanding and embracing the values, beliefs, and goals in place; and (c) fully under-standing and embracing the nature of relationships, even as they apply to time and nature. Schein, best known as one of MIT's professors and an expert in organizational development, also provided a formal definition of culture: "A pattern of shared basic assumptions that the group learned as it solved its problems of external adaptation and internal integration that has worked well enough to be considered valid and, therefore, to be taught to new members as the correct way to perceive, think, and feel in relation to those problems."[24]

In layman's terms, culture is "how we do things around here." The three principles from Schein help us to unravel this mystery of the Nutro culture, and how its members made that magic happen.

Artifacts and Actions

Artifacts include everything we see about the company—the rituals, the lingo, symbols, and even how people dress. The Nutro culture was able to create a powerful impact using symbols, one of which we see in Figure 17.

Figure 17: Photo of a Japanese manufacturer in Tokyo.
Source: Christie Cooper.

The photo, taken of a Japanese pet food manufacturer in Tokyo, shows how one culture can influence another. Normally, Japan has an elaborate code for etiquette. When I traveled to Japan to work with this team, I'd been warned that a training class there would not be the same as it is in the United States. I was told to prepare for blank stares and no questions. Yet this photo clearly depicts an interaction that has relaxed into something like a skit from *Saturday Night Live*—reminding us of Steve Martin and Dan Ackroyd's "wild and crazy guys"! This lighthearted demeanor rarely happens in Japanese corporate training.

Another example of this lightheartedness has to do with a rubber chicken. Since it was critical for Nutro to convey their most valued strategy—product ingredient differential—they did this by calling on "the power of the chicken." Employees used a rubber chicken containing guts made of yarn to show the differential. It might sound a little hokey, but Nutro put chicken meal on the map of success. As discussed in the previous chapter, while P&G, Colgate Palmolive, Nestle, and Purina were using by-products, Nutro made sure the consumer saw the *value* of chicken meal—an ingredient with a premium price. In fact, it was essentially the same chicken that consumers purchased in the grocery store to put on the dinner table for their families—just with the water and fat removed. Cost was not a consideration at Nutro. Using pricier ingredients and their formulation contributed to the products' value—and ultimate success.

The rubber chicken was a marketing item the sales team could order just as they ordered brochures. A Nutro manager who gave his or her sales team a recipe for success might provide something like this as part of the "rubber chicken" demonstration:

Recipe, Part 1: Gain Recommendation
Ingredients needed:

- ☐ 1 rubber chicken
- ☐ 1 pair of scissors
- ☐ 1 safety razor
- ☐ 1 dog food bowl
- ☐ 1 trash can
- ☐ 1 Bic lighter
- ☐ 3 feet of laundry dryer duct about 6–8 inches in diameter
- ☐ 1 miniature chicken on a key chain

Instructions:

In front of a comfortably seated audience, sitting upon stacks of dog food displays or a fifty-pound container of cat litter, begin using your props to engage the audience. First, ask them what they feed their dog or cat. Make a mental note if most are feeding something with by-products in it. Ask the audience: If they found a food with better ingredients—would they feed it to their pets? The answer is always "yes" (unless someone is a jokester).

Next, place the dog food bowl on the tabletop object for all to see. Pick up the rubber chicken and ask for a volunteer. Hand scissors to the volunteer and ask them to cut off the chicken's head and feet. Have the volunteer discard these "ingredients" into the dog food bowl. Next, have them pick up the safety razor and make an incision in the belly of the chicken. Then, have them remove the guts from chicken (the yarn) and discard into the bowl with the other parts of chicken.

The main point to make is this: The heads, feet, and guts are by-products. Would you feed this to your family? The answer is always no. Use a mixture of other emphatic words and phrases to indicate "how gross this is!" Next, remove the by-products from the dog bowl and place remaining "chicken body" in the now-empty dog food bowl. This is fresh chicken. Which would you rather feed your family? How about your pet?

Recipe, Part 2:

Thank the current volunteer and have them sit down. Ask for two new volunteers. Have each hold up an end of the dryer duct. Have Volunteer A place the chicken body inside the dryer duct. Using the Bic lighter, flick the flame on under the dryer duct as if you are "cooking the chicken." Take a miniature chicken on a key chain out of your pocket, discreetly hand it to Volunteer B, and have them take the tiny chicken out of the dryer duct instead. Say, "It went in as chicken and weighed more; once that chicken was cooked, it cooked out the water and fat and the end product was much smaller in size and weight." State emphatically, "It takes five pounds of fresh chicken to make one pound of chicken meal." Ask the audience: "What is the key takeaway?" There is more chicken in chicken meal than in fresh, whole chicken!

This trick was just one of many used to talk about the "differential." Employees used this play out of the Nutro playbook repeatedly over the years as the company grew—from 9 salespeople in 1986, to 150 in 1996, to almost 300 salespeople by the year 2004. Consistency became a part of the strategy. The artifacts or props that employees utilized had increased from just rubber chickens and chicken on a key chain to chicken ties, chicken hats, white chicken lab coats, and even chicken necklaces (Figure 18). Salespeople used these artifacts to help drive the messaging on Nutro's use of top-notch ingredients.

Figure 18: Photo of Japanese
manufacturer in Tokyo.
Source: Christie Cooper.

Photos like the one above were commonly taken of Nutro seminar attendees. People wanted to belong to this group called Nutro, whose members brought infectious excitement and fun to others. One European salesperson even went so far as to name Nutro's cultural wackiness "the Nutro Virus." This individual showed up to a national sales meeting with virus-themed stickers that he distributed to everyone in the audience. The members promptly placed the stickers on the name badges hanging around their necks. It was great to see our European counterparts so passionate about the products we were selling in the States.

The Nutro Virus was infectious. Before long, it was spreading quickly; and Nutro was growing sales—*fast.*

Values, Beliefs, and Goals

In 2016, we surveyed over one hundred Nutro employees and asked them to use adjectives to describe the culture of the organization. From this list of words, we get a glimpse into the inner workings of an organization that created not only a community, but also a family (Figure 19).

Family Hard Fun Competitive Passionate

Figure 19: Word cloud of adjectives used
to describe the culture of Nutro.

Fun. Most people don't automatically associate this word with their jobs—but having fun at work *is* important. Dr. David Abramis, a researcher on methods of creating highly motivating workplaces, found that people who have fun at work are more productive, more creative, make better decisions, and get along better with their colleagues. They're less likely to be late, and they have fewer absences—a win-win for both company and the employee.[25]

While "fun" was not an outcome that Nutro's founders intentionally set out to create, it happened organically. Employees experienced fun in a variety of ways, from wins at retail to the biannual sales meetings the company held. These meetings, Tahoe and Christmas, were one way that owner Dave Traitel used to inspire and thank his team and their families. The Lake Tahoe meeting was held in June. The crisp, clean air and greenery offered a refreshing break from the daily grind of selling the World's Best Pet Food. Getting to Tahoe after working the first five months of the year was a nice break—and from the sales team's perspective, the trip was even sweeter if they'd accomplished their sales goals throughout the year. May and November were historically the months with the highest sales goals and revenue generation. No one wanted to show up to a sales meeting having not made the months prior to the meeting. The sales regions would have the grit and determination to bring home the number in these months.

Everyone in the company worked hard, and everyone played hard in Lake Tahoe. The owner provided an "outing allowance" to each employee—a small stipend to participate in any activity they wanted the day before the sales meeting. These activities ranged from going to the spa for a massage, hang gliding, boating, canoeing, hiking, renting dirt bikes, and others. It was the owner's way of saying, "Thank you for all you do"—in a heartfelt way that employees appreciated. People participated in these activities with their teammates, which further strengthened team rapport and relationships.

"Work hard and play hard" was certainly a motto that many at Nutro believed in and celebrated. A lot of the opportunities to celebrate, talk shop, and catch up happened at Rookies, the local sports bar in North Shore Lake Tahoe. Usually, the Canadian team became most competitive in drinking games while playing foosball or billiards. Indeed, their fierce, almost warriorlike attitude came through in their substantial sales increases year over year. One of the best IT support folks explained it as follows: "Nutro led the natural pet food industry, and the sales division led Nutro. What sales wanted, sales got. Marketing and R&D, sparsely populated departments, existed to serve the insatiable demands of one of the last feet-in-the-street selling machines. It was almost a cult, stuffed to the rafters as it were with high-octane, hard-drinking, road-warrior, half-crazy salesmen and women."

The Christmas meeting was truly a very special and memorable week. Spouses were invited to attend, and the company covered all travel costs. The trip created closeness between both colleagues and families. Spouses attended a luncheon and toured during the first day of the sales meeting, while employees participated in the meeting.

The highlight of the Christmas meeting was certainly the Christmas party. No expense was spared. Once the company became big enough, the Christmas party moved from the home of David and Joan Traitel to the Jonathan Club, a political club established in 1895 that had evolved into a social club. Up until nearly the late 1980s, this club's membership was men only. Women attending the Nutro sales meeting had to be escorted by a male member around the facilities.

Eventually, company executives sought out another setting for the party and chose the Ritz-Carlton in San Marino, California, as the new—very nice, and very upscale—Christmas meeting venue. Formal business attire was required, although a suit and tie seemed like overkill for this rather casual company. People who were skilled in encouraging audience participation were always a highlight of the meeting. These people would conduct a mini-seminar for the audience, which normally contained many newbies.

One such skit was reminiscent of a Gallagher comedy act. Leo Gallagher was a comedian known for using props as a part of his act. In particular, he was fond whacking open watermelons with a very large mallet. So one afternoon for the mini-seminar breakout session, a manager from the Midwest conducted a similar act, requiring the two front rows to wear inexpensive rain gear (actually, just garbage bags with holes cut out for people's heads). Now remember—all of this was taking place at the *Ritz-Carlton*. The thick, plush, cream-colored carpet—along with the drapes and the white tablecloths—was soon soaked with watermelon chunks, seeds, and juice. It was a mess. That was the last meeting we had at the Ritz—which probably wasn't a coincidence.

Either because we outgrew the Ritz (or weren't allowed to return), Palm Springs became the new home of the December national meeting. The surroundings were much more relaxed and casual, and therefore a much better fit with the company's culture.

Family. This was the second-most frequently used word when describing the culture. The owner's generosity, and the way he made those in his organization feel like they were *his* family, was central to this company. It is instinctual to want to take care of and defend your family—and Dave protected his flock. His generosity extended to even preparing and cooking the meat at the manufacturing plant company BBQ. Dave knew everyone and acknowledged everyone. There are numerous stories of individuals who were facing tough personal issues, including medical conditions. Situations ranged from kidney transplants to alcohol abuse to funeral arrangements. Dave Traitel subsidized many of these situations. One employee shares his gratitude, saying: "Nutro was a company who truly cared about their people. During my tenure with Nutro, I was diagnosed with multiple sclerosis and was unable to work. I received nothing but compassion during this difficult time. I received calls from [my manager] checking in on me regularly and reassuring me that Nutro [would] always have a place for me, for as long as it [took]. [He only cared] about my well-being . . . Nutro continued to pay me to ensure that my family and I didn't suffer any further hardship. I truly believe that this played a vital role in my recovery and [allowed me to] return to work after three months. I will forever be grateful!"

Esprit de corps—a feeling of pride, fellowship, and common loyalty—was apparent at national sales meetings. In particular, two events were highly recognized by survey respondents: the Annual Chili Cook-off and the Pet Food Peddler. The Annual Chili Cook-off was held in June during the Lake Tahoe national meeting. Each of the six regions created its own theme and assembled its booth. Regions generally assigned a small team to develop a concept or idea that would be the basis for all costumes or attire that the region's team would wear. The Southwest region (Figure 20) went so far as to create a skit based on the movie *Wyatt Earp*. (You might notice the holstered guns on the hips of the individuals below. The hotel's security department was notified of the use of these child's guns as props!)

Figure 20: Annual Chili Cook-off.
Pictured from left to right: Scott Keller, Frank
Hon, Greg Hutsell, and Don Carlson.
Photo credit: Christie Cooper.

Each region turned in their chili recipe to Peggy Pennington, Dave Traitel's administrative assistant and the ultimate meeting planner. Peggy ensured that everyone received all the chili ingredients they needed. Each region elected a chef, who then picked others to help in the preparation. One region arranged an impromptu team meeting in advance of the Tahoe sales meeting to serve various chilis that were then voted on. The winning recipe was served to the judges at the Tahoe Chili Cook-off (Figure 21).

Nutro made a competition out of everything—and the Chili Cook-off was no different. Employees cherished this face-to-face time. As one employee shared, "I miss Nutro . . . miss Tahoe and Palm Springs, and I miss the friendships. I keep connected via Facebook and LinkedIn, but there was just something about those semiannual sales meetings. Serious bonding went on there. They were like family reunions."

Figure 21: Annual Chili Cook-off judging.
Pictured from left to right: Dave Kravis, Jerry Sicherman,
Ladd Hardy, Mike Satterwhite, and Dave Traitel.
Photo credit: Lori Thomas.

The feeling of family was so strong that no matter where someone was, they wanted to be sure that consumers had the opportunity to belong to the Nutro family by feeding their pets the product. Competitors saw this as a cult mentality. Those inside the company knew others were saying this, but it was more than okay with them; it was a really a badge of honor, according to one employee: "Nutro was a family and became part of your identity. In addition to [encouraging] personal goal setting, it created an intense team-based program that held you accountable [to both yourself and to others]. We created a cultlike phenomenon behind an industry-leading product."

Passionate. For those who worked inside the company, the word *passionate* comes up frequently. *Passion* conveys an intense love of the product, and the view that any other product was inferior. Nutro team members went to great lengths to share their love for the products they sold. Passion extended beyond the product; people were passionate about *each other*. Team members felt an incredible sense of camaraderie: "[There was an] environment of internal competition along with feeling like a band of brothers and sisters—coupled with an incredible selling story that, at the time, competitors could not rival. And somehow, [Nutro had] the ability to find the most amazing people to work within the industry. They were not just bodies with order pads and a set of car keys. They were, and still are . . . the gold standard of associates. The truly passionate amongst us, no matter when they became part of the Nutro family, treated the brand as if it were their own child. We were passionate about the brand and knew that its' success reflected directly on ourselves and our success." As another leader tells it, Nutro was "an energetic and confident company with a passion and drive rarely seen. Great people, all of whom were incredibly charismatic and great *leaders* of people."

Everyone who worked at the company displayed an entrepreneurial spirit. Plenty of people said that being a salesperson at Nutro was the next closest thing to owning your own business. Each salesperson felt empowered to treat their territory as if it *was* truly their business—and that's what they often did.

Competitive. Nutro created and delivered rewards in a way that encouraged competition. The friendly rivalry started out among only a few individuals in the early days. Later on, when the company had six regions across the US including Canada, competition became much fiercer. Everyone who worked at Nutro had an incredible will to win, to succeed, and never give up. This desire for success changed many individuals' personal lives. One employee comments on what it was like to work during his tenure: "Our goal was not simply to sell dog food, but to convert the minds and hearts of every consumer, retail associate, buyer, family member, and so on. We loved to be hated by every competitor. Gunslingers deal in lead; we dealt in kibble, and there wasn't another company around who could put us down. We were the outlaw and the sheriff, and we owned not just Main Street—but the whole town."

Regardless of their department, each team member had a sense of pride about their work and their company.

Hard work. Anyone in the pet industry would likely agree that Nutro employed the hardest-working individuals between 1975 and 2007. If an employee did not exemplify hard work, they did not last long. Management expected their teams to put in long hours. Some might say that Nutro employees made great sacrifices by being away from their families to achieve the company's goals; however, this hard work was not something that Nutro workers saw as a sacrifice, since everyone on the team—even down to the warehouse workers—received a bonus. Everyone loved or at least cared deeply for one another; as mentioned previously, most felt that working at Nutro was almost like owning their own businesses. We gave our sweat, heart, and tears to make the company successful. When the competitors ended their day, many Nutro employees would still be out at their retail stores—selling promotions, setting up displays, or educating store employees after hours. We didn't have to be told to do this; we just did it. As one salesperson explains, the competition wanted to be like Nutro: "The feeling of family and enthusiasm for making and selling the world's best dog food we had during our sales meetings, and the competitive spirit we had during the early days of the pet food peddler competition . . . these are two things that pet companies today try to emulate."

Nature of relationships. Relationships—between both internal and external customers—were vital to the organization's success. There were certainly personality conflicts from time to time, and of course, egos occasionally got in the way—as is bound to happen at any company. But most employees enjoyed the people they worked for *and* with. It's an amazing thing to be able to go to work and love what you do. Working with people with whom you have such a strong bond makes for an even more incredible experience.

The competition tried hard to mimic what Nutro was doing out in the field with retailers and consumers, and I suppose that would be the highest form of flattery. However, it was a difficult task for the competition to actually *do* what we did. Some organizations out there today, such as Disneyland and Zappos, offer "university" type training. For example, individuals and companies can go to Zappos to learn what makes their culture and customer service unique. People can sign up for the Zappos Culture Camp, pay $6,000, and learn about core values, on-boarding new employees, creating employee engagement and happiness, and hiring for a culture fit. And if you don't care to spend that much money, you can at least check out their culture book.[26] The culture at Zappos is the closest we have seen to our experience at Nutro. They begin with clearly stated values and goals. Their team works hard together to achieve these goals, then celebrates together as well.

Celebrations are another critical component to creating this kind of desired culture. Celebrating success can be a challenge in today's global landscape because of remote work teams, but that's no reason to omit this essential step. Reveling in success and wins guarantees that your teams will become closer. This small investment can have rather large dividends, and it's helpful to have a reminder or memento of these celebrations! As one former Nutro employee explains, "I still carry my Nutro key chain I received in my first meeting twenty-five plus years ago. Ed Brown and this company gave me an opportunity of a lifetime that took me to places and exposed me to things I would have never done on my own . . . Through it all, it was the time of my life and my career."

Nutro taught us and countless other employees the importance of creating and nurturing a winning culture. While each company has its own degree or formality (or lack of it), consider how important the following elements are when building your own winning culture:

1. Create a **simple vision** that the people in the organization can understand and rally behind. This allows them to be truly passionate about the cause a company is working toward. For

Nutro, it was simple: "Sell the world's best pet food, one bag at a time."

2. Encourage an **entrepreneurial spirit**. People want freedom and autonomy. When is the last time you heard someone say, "I'd prefer to be micromanaged"? Give people the tools to do their job—then get out of their way. Empowerment is one of those effective tools, so use it. For the Nutro employees, in particular the sales team, their job was the closest thing to owning their own business—and they treated it that way.

3. Keep in mind that there is no replacement for **hard work**—which at times can translate into long hours. But it can also translate into finding new processes and productivity streams that get the work done more efficiently. Hard work is also an attitude—one that does not stop until the person undergoing the endeavor obtains his or her goal.

4. Remember the "**with whom**" connection. Taking a journey with someone whom you can really depend on is critical. Being able to love your job and go to work is one aspect; being able to call those you work with *family* is what creates a tightknit team. This teamwork then becomes the competitive advantage. Organizations can observe this cultural climate in other companies; yet the process of carrying it out poses different challenges. We'll look more closely at how Nutro did this in the next chapter.

CHAPTER 12: CATALYSTS TO SUCCESS: THE PRODUCT

"Success is walking from failure to failure without loss of enthusiasm."

—Winston Churchill

Numerous small wins contributed to Nutro's success; however, this chapter will focus on what we call The Big 5, which covers two main aspects: product and people. In this chapter, we will discuss product—specifically the two main product launches that moved the company toward prominence. Chapter 12 will discuss the people—specifically, the three components that made Nutro's people such a critical part of the company's success.

We used qualitative research in the form of online surveys and in-person interviews as a way to collect data from all teams within the organization—manufacturing, operations, sales, marketing, administration, human resources, R&D, and accounting. Each of these departments contributed to the goal of "selling one bag at a time" and improving the lives of pets. The areas of greatest success involved product creation, building a team, and retailer support. Let's look at each of these in detail.

Product Creation: Max

In 1985, after several unsuccessful attempts to create a new product called Max Stress, Sharon Machlik—whom we first introduced in Chapter 6—joined the team at Nutro. Sharon had originally been hired to make a cat food line. However, Max Stress had been not finding success with its formulation, so Sharon was transitioned over to reformulate and reinvigorate the dog food line. In doing so, Max Stress was renamed simply Max.

Max's unique makeup was an innovative blend of chicken, rice, and lamb. Dr. Machlik collaborated with Dr. Peter Ihrke, a veterinarian from UC Davis, whose expertise in companion animal dermatology is unmatched and highly regarded. While we don't have all the specifics of this working relationship, we do know that Dr. Ihrke had a significant impact on Dr. Machlik's ability to impart successful recipes formulated for a healthy skin and coat. In fact, Nutro patented this "formulated for healthy skin and coat" claim, along with the exact recipe. This claim gave credence to Max and subsequent Nutro foods. Dr. Machlik helped ensure the food was bulletproof for the team who steadfastly sold the products.

Product Creation: Natural Choice Lamb and Rice

In the late 1990s, an important debate was taking place within the company. Nature's Recipe was gaining shelf space, and sales grew steadily for them in a new category of pet food: lamb and rice. Sales wanted the product, but marketing was skeptical; and select members of the executive team were strongly opposed to creating a product in this new category. Max dog food was selling well, and Nutro employees were concerned that they would cannibalize their own sales. Months passed without an agreement. Finally in 1991, after much continued debate, the internal teams reached a consensus to formulate Natural Choice Lamb and Rice.

The product gained instant success. Timing could not have been better, as Nutro had one edge over Nature's Recipe now: Natural Choice was formulated with rice, and Nature's Recipe used wheat. This made all the difference. Nutro continued to gain momentum, while sales for Nature's Recipe soon came to a dead stop. Nature's Recipe became contaminated with a vomitoxin, a substance found in wet grain that occurs while food is being transported by rail car across the country. Companies that conduct in-house ingredient testing can easily detect vomitoxins and other health hazards for pets, but something went awry for Nature's Recipe. A massive recall during the mid-1990s forced them to take all their product off the shelves. It was surprising that they were able to rebound at all after this.

The Nutro sales team took full advantage of the Nature's Recipe mistake. They were able to gain new placement for Natural Choice Lamb and Rice, since stores needed something to replace the faulty Nature's Recipe product. Soon, Natural Choice Lamb and Rice became the company's cash cow.

CHAPTER 13: CATALYSTS TO SUCCESS: TAKING A NEW INITIATIVE

"Risk comes from not knowing what you're doing."

—Warren Buffett

Three particular steps contributed most potently to the organization's acceleration: the demo team, leaving, and then returning to the big giant—otherwise known as PetSmart.

Building a Demo Team

The purpose of this tactic was to educate, promote, and convert consumers who were using other pet food products. Nutro was the first to develop such a unique marketing strategy in the pet industry. The demo program started in 1982, with less than fifteen demonstrators throughout Southern California. The goal was to reach as many consumers as possible who came through the front door of pet specialty stores—including military exchanges, commissaries, and various consumer shows. A demonstrator worked a shift, generally on the weekend, with the aim of telling the Nutro story and trying to sell a bag of pet food to as many customers as possible.

Each salesperson targeted the top-ten stores in their territory, and tracked each one's progress. The goal was always to take our *unfair share*—a term used to denote the gain of market share, shelf space, and recommendation that Nutro seized from the competition. Ultimately, each account grew one bag—and one consumer—at a time.

Nutro did not have the funds the large conglomerates had to invest in television, magazines, large consumer booths, and free product samples. Procter & Gamble, Colgate Palmolive, Nestle, Purina, and Pedigree spent the lion's share on TV advertising that drove consumers to the pet stores. Then, Nutro was present and ready in stores, happy to convert those consumers face-to-face.

Nutro was able to share their bulletproof story of "No Heads, No Feet, No Guts; Feed Less, Poop Less, and Shed Less." Demonstrators were equipped with demo tables that looked like actual product displays. The demo team utilized the same props the sales team used while conducting their seminars—that infamous rubber chicken, along with chicken heads, feet, feces, and guts (yarn) coming out of the dogs' bowl to represent to consumers what they might be feeding their dogs. Charts comparing Nutro to as many as ten other brands provided a visual aid for consumers and allowed them to see what ingredients Nutro used versus their competitors. During their four hour shifts, Nutro demonstrators educated store workers and empowered them to recommend the products to new consumers seven days a week. The math was simple: Convert ten new customers a week, who then told ten new people about the product—and the retailer would have hundreds of new customers in a matter of months and new orders to place with distributors. As one Nutro employee emphasized, "Education was a big part of the marketing. The demo program was invaluable. Teaching consumers about the ingredients was so important to Nutro's success."

Initially, district managers—the outside salespeople—managed their demo staff and demo programs. They would pick their target stores and hire the staff. Some district managers had as many as twenty-five or thirty demonstrators, in addition to their normal duties of selling, merchandising, and educating all the retailers in their own territory. Much was expected of the sales team, who worked harder and longer than the competitors most likely worked.

As Nutro grew, company leaders truly came to appreciate the importance of the demo program and its growth potential. They decided to hire staff specifically to oversee the demonstrators, and give some relief to the district managers (DMs). This allowed the DMs to spend more time selling the product to the stores; in turn, the demo team would push the product out the front door.

Not surprisingly, the big conglomerates did not like Nutro. As the company gained a positive reputation via word of mouth, and as sales started to grow, competitors felt the strain. But Nutro was unstoppable. The demonstrators were well trained and continued to hold monthly demo meetings. Each demonstrator's line manager would go out and work with them in the field to assist with any issues or difficulties they faced in converting consumers, and district managers would assist in field training as well. In fact, many DMs were a large source of motivation and inspiration for the demonstrators. As shown in the photo, trying to make the job fun was an important aspect for them (Figure 22).

Figure 22
Pictured from left to right: Unnamed
PetSmart store manager; Aaron
Schmidt, demo manager; PetSmart
store manager; Lia Rivadeneyra, DM.
Photo credit: Christie Cooper.

Nutro's demo program became the example for other companies. Yet no matter how hard the competition tried to mimic this element of Nutro's success, they were never able to do it as well. In fact, other pet food companies feared the program so much they tried many different ways to stop Nutro's approach—the most prevalent form being lawsuits. Soon, Nutro found itself constantly defending the program and their demo team. Too frequently, David Traitel's little company was locked in a heated battle between Colgate Palmolive and Procter & Gamble. But Traitel did not care if he spent more money in legal fees than the settlement he had expected to win. He just wanted the "big guys" to lose.

Demonstrators commonly educated consumers on ingredients, specifically by comparing ingredients and products. They taught store staff, vets, dog trainers, and new pet owners. Nutro trained pet parents how to read the labels of the product they were feeding their pets, and how to compare the ingredients, feeding levels, waste production, and skin and coat results. The most important advice demonstrators gave was how to "make the switch" in a way that would help prevent pets from experiencing temporary digestive upset.

Nutro's demo program launched in the early 1980s with just a handful of demo staff. By the beginning of 1993, three full-time territory demo managers (TDMs) wrote manuals on hiring, training, scheduling, and handling issues with the new and growing demo program. This documentation was carefully created to assist future employees in following the recipe for success. Later on, the company hired a TDM for each state, each of whom was responsible for hundreds of demo staff. By 2007, Nutro had over 3,500 part-time demonstrators converting and selling their products consistently across the United States, Canada, and Europe.

The company was always pushing the envelope to educate as many customers as possible on the product's many benefits. Nutro offered solutions to their pets' age, weight, large breed, small breed, allergy, and grain-free needs—and of course, Nutro helped pets with skin and coat issues. Nutro taught their demonstrators to be bold in approaching customers; you could often find them roaming the store and walking competitors' aisles with the mission to start a conversation. Nutro's demo team took pet food nutrition to a new level by learning as much as they could about the competition's products.

The TDMs would conduct monthly demo meetings to highlight top accounts and top demo staff, and to discuss what the team could do better to gain more new consumers and sales. The demonstrators felt appreciated, supported, and empowered; they were entrepreneurs of their program. They knew the growth that was occurring in stores was because of *their* hard work, high conversions, and sales.

Nutro began using demonstrators at dog, cat, and consumer shows if the DM was unable to attend. The demo team members served as the voice of the customers; they were able to see what was going on in the marketplace and report on it. Pet shows provided yet another source of information on what consumers were looking for. Demonstrators soon learned about what ingredients consumers wanted and did not want, and they pushed this information up through the company's top tiers. Nutro created many new items based on the feedback that demonstrators gathered directly from customers.

The demo team learned about upcoming promotions, product launches, and other intel that store managers were happy to share with their beloved Nutro demonstrators. As such, Nutro received firsthand information on the competitors' marketing and promotional calendars. The store staff saw the Nutro demonstrator as part of *their* store team, and therefore volunteered early information on competitors' new product launches, product failures, and ingredient changes.

This positive word of mouth went beyond just store employees. Dog groomers recommended the product to the hundreds of clients they saw monthly. The demo team gave dog trainers free samples of pet food and treats to pass out to their clients. One bag at a time and one consumer conversion at a time equaled thousands of bags a month of new growth as the fantastic team of demonstrators grew. Nutro's demo team was a well-oiled machine, and retailers came to see their demonstrators as a great resource.

CHAPTER 14: CATALYSTS TO SUCCESS: TAKING A BIG PLUNGE

"The first step toward success is taken when you refuse to be a captive of the environment in which you first find yourself."

—Mark Caine

Retailer Support: Divorced from PetSmart

In 1995, after several years of partnering and conducting business with PetSmart, Nutro decided to dissolve their relationship with the mega pet retailer. As of 2016, PetSmart had 1,466 locations in the United States, Canada, and Puerto Rico, and 53,000 store associates. Back in 1992, the fiftieth PetSmart store had just opened in the United States.[27] At the time, Nutro felt it was not receiving the support it needed from the large retailer. So after much consideration, Dave Traitel insisted that Nutro withdraw from their organization. Back then, PetSmart operated as more of a grocery store for pets. There was little interaction between consumer and employee, which meant that PetSmart did not appreciate the benefit of

Nutro's demo program—or allow it to thrive. As a result, all ties between the organizations were severed.

The "divorce letter," dated May 29, 1995, was distributed to the Nutro sales team, giving full transparency to the communication between Nutro and PetSmart. Essentially the letter shared the substantial disagreements between the two companies. The irreconcilable differences stemmed from differences in philosophy; Nutro wanted to conduct demos in their stores, and PetSmart did not want to allow it. The last order was shipped to PetSmart on July 1, 1992, at which time the relationship was amicably severed. Later a senior representative of PetSmart retorted back with a sharp tongue, stating, "Maybe our pets are better off without Nutro's products and philosophy." A short while later, PetSmart created their own house brand called Authority, which they attempted to sell to Nutro customers. It is both authors' opinion, along with many others in the industry, that Authority was created to help reduce their own gap in sales. Loyal Nutro customers soon found themselves shopping at other stores.

This was a very bold move on Nutro's part. Company executives didn't feel that the direction in which PetSmart was going at the time—to a warehouse club feel with a focus on low prices—was the direction in which Nutro was heading. Often, the mega store would sell the product for under cost and use certain "lost leaders" to gain traction. All the while, small independently owned pet and feed stores were suffering the wrath of the then-discount giant.

Ironically, Nutro received a letter from a Petco senior vice president acknowledging Nutro's contributions to making 1994 Petco's most successful year to date. Nutro was recognized for playing a big part in this sales increase.

So the team continued to focus on doing what it did best—selling one bag at a time—while supporting a new mantra: "No PetSmart." This refrain gained the still-growing pet food company much traction with independently owned pet specialty stores. As such, the sales team put all their focus and energy into this segment of the market. The team created tight-knit relationships with their customers and worked hard on their behalf to increase sales. Nutro's sales steadily grew, while they continued to gain support and recommendation from retailers throughout the US and the world.

Code Name Monica: Paired Back Up with PetSmart

Marketing consultant partner Annamarie Turano wrote this for the Retail Customer Experience group: "Price is not where PetSmart plays; lower prices can easily be found at Walmart, Target, and online specialty retailers. However, PetSmart's focus on trusted care minimizes the importance of price in the minds of pet owners."[28] This statement conveys the shift that the mega retailer eventually made from low-cost leader to pet parent supporter.

Government covert operations all seem to have secret code names—like the Acoustic Kitty, a CIA project from the '60s trying to use cats to spy on Soviet embassies; or the more famous Bay of Pigs, an unsuccessful invasion of Cuba. Well, Nutro had its own code name for going back to PetSmart. They called it "Monica." You might wonder—why Monica? Well, it was around the time that President Clinton had an inappropriate relationship with an intern named Monica Lewinsky. Clandestine meetings were arranged between Nutro and PetSmart executives to discuss entering back into a relationship. According to a Nutro marketing executive, "Both companies went so far as to check in with fictitious names and we never stayed at the same hotel twice." Seems as though President Clinton and Nutro were both hiding relationships from the public.

By refocusing their goals and strategy, PetSmart regained Nutro's support—and the two companies strategically decided to "date" again. By 1999, Nutro received placement back on PetSmart's shelves. And by that time, those fifty stores had grown to over five hundred.[29] Nutro continued to revel in double-digit growth.

CHAPTER 15: LESSONS LEARNED: DEDICATED TO ENTREPRENEURS

"Never look back unless you are planning to go that way."

—Henry David Thoreau

I can still hear my mom telling me, "Sweetie, you need to learn from my mistakes. Don't make the same mistakes I did." Most kids don't care to hear this; after all, we think, *How much do my parents know?* However, the experiences from people who worked at Nutro can serve to help other companies and entrepreneurs. These insights and perceptions from individuals inside the company should serve as lessons learned. It's truly a chance to learn from our mistakes.

So—what *were* some of these mistakes?

Everyone Is a Zebra

In other words—everyone looked the same. The organization was very homogeneous and lacked diversity. Look at this classic picture from the 1960s (Figure 23). Compare it to the next photo (Figure 24), which shows a group of millennials enrolled at California State University who are involved in the Sales Leadership Center, earning bachelor's degrees and professional sales certificates. Diversity has increased over the last sixty years.

Figure 23: WWPSA Meeting. John Saleen is
pictured in the back row on the right.
Source unknown.

Figure 24: CSUF sales leadership team.
Photo Credit: Mark Mantey, codirector of the Sales Leadership Center.

Gender Bias

This is another element that these two photos clearly demonstrate. During the '60s, the workplace was still very much a place for men; they were the breadwinners, while women took care of the household. This type of cultural norm meant that organizations often overlooked women, didn't see them as equals—and therefore rejected them for senior-type management positions. Up until May 2007, a female never held the role of president, vice president, or any other C-suite positions at Nutro. While several female individuals were an integral part of the business and certainly carried much clout, none received the appropriate or deserved C-suite title. This was not something people perceived as unusual back in the 1970s and '80s. It was, unfortunately, the norm.

This pattern continued to pervade the organization. Some of the women and men who we interviewed for this book shared their disappointment in the lack of diversity and equality between males and females. One senior executive seemed to feel sincere remorse and shame over not hiring one particular female to run the manufacturing facility, especially since she was probably even more qualified than the male counterpart who interviewed for the same position.

Things were especially hard for working mothers. Bearing the burden and joy of child rearing while juggling the demands of the job was quite difficult at times. Women at Nutro had to work just as hard—which meant just as long—as their male counterparts in order to be seen as successful. Whether male or female, demonstrating a robust work ethic, a drive for results, and a sense of resilience were all requirements to succeed.

There is a great deal of debate regarding equal pay for men and women in the workplace nowadays, and questions about why women *still* don't earn as much as their male counterparts. Women's roles as caregivers in raising children might come into play here; there was certainly a concern at Nutro around women being able to do the same work a man could. If a woman took on a particular role, management worried she might become pregnant—and then wondered how much she'd be able to work. This out-look ended up creating a very homogenous company comprised of mostly male, Caucasian employees between thirty and fifty years of age—with only slight variation. A 2011 study conducted by McKinsey & Company found that only about 14 percent of women make up top executive committees in Fortune 500 companies, and very few CEOs are female.[30] Some individuals who worked at Nutro expressed deep regret for potentially overlooking a woman for a role due to her gender.

Technology

Technology was never one of Nutro's strong suits. There's a well-known story from the mid-1980s about the company's decision to purchase a fax machine. It was amazing how something seemingly so small could create such discussion! From the '70s to the early '90s, fax machines and cell phones were nonexistent. The debate about increasing the company's technology resources grew—and became rather heated. If material needed to travel between departments, employees frequently used Federal Express—without much thought to the cost. At some point, this caught up to employees—and the first corporate office fax machine was purchased. (A thermal paper fax machine, no less!). Having a fax machine soon created "fax envy" among senior leaders and departments.

The organization wasn't much of a leader in other tech-related areas. Most companies today consider technology to be something to "lean into." A study by MIT Sloan Management Review and Capgemini Consulting "finds that companies [having more than $1 billion in revenues] now face a digital imperative: adopt new technologies effectively or face competitive obsolescence."[31] This advice will likely prove instrumental for the pet industry as well, especially since e-commerce now represents one of the fastest growing segments in the pet channel. According to a Nielsen global pet food study (2015), E-commerce accounted for 2 percent of the global sales in 2013. The US represented the largest of eight countries leading this pace.[32]

CHAPTER 16: MEMORIES

"Nothing is ever really lost to us as long as we remember it."

—L.M. Montgomery

Memories that previous team members have shared have been extremely helpful to us in writing this book. We're grateful to hear former Nutro employees' heartfelt insights and stories, and have tried to the best of our ability to capture this feedback. People made all sorts of telling comments—in face-to-face interviews, phone interviews, or via an online survey—when describing their time at Nutro. Including:

- The most fun and professionally rewarding time in my career.
- An energetic and confident company with a passion and drive rarely seen. Great people, all of whom were incredibly charismatic and great leaders of individuals.
- The most fantastic company you could ever work for!
- One of the best experiences of my life. I will never forget the time I worked here. It had a significant impact on my career.

- High energy, demanding, fun, a once in a life experience. I miss it ... and everyone ...

- Intangible spirit that permeated the Nutro sales force that drove us to new heights.

- Fast paced, hard work, and we didn't know how good we were as a team. The likes will never be duplicated again in the pet industry, or others.

- The best experience of my life and a real jolt into the very competitive pet trade.

- A life-changing event in every way.

It's been a privilege to capture the hearts and minds of the team members that have worked for the company. Make no mistake: The company was not perfect. After all, no company is. However, many of us indeed experienced what we truly felt was a version of Camelot. For this, we all must thank our fearless leader, David Traitel (Figure 25).

Figure 25: Nutro's fearless leader, Dave Traitel.
Photo Credit: Christie Cooper.

People use a variety of kind words to describe Dave—humble, genuine, and an authentic leader. He is a charming man of the utmost integrity. The honesty and integrity he has always displayed are competencies that are necessary for a successfully and inspiring leader. Dave exudes these, and he has always sought the truth. He managed to be a man of great strength and fortitude, yet at the same time, always very approachable. He believed in hiring the best people and then staying out of their way. He gave each person the autonomy they needed. According to one employee, "[Nutro was] a true family-owned company where the owner valued his employees. The workers treated the company like it was [their] own business."

Dave was present at each national meeting, warmly greeting those entering and leaving the conference. A man of great generosity and selflessness, he sought to make the lives of pets better by providing "the best pet food in the world"—and enriching the lives of those he employed as well.

Dave demanded excellence and people gave it. He demanded hard work and people gave it. He demanded loyalty and *he* gave it.

In 2013, David T. Traitel was the recipient of the Uncommon Commitment Award, an honor given to individuals making outstanding contributions to the Hoover Institution. To further demonstrate the Traitel family's commitment to the Hoover Institution, a wing named after David and Joan Traitel is expected to be completed sometime in 2017.

To close this chapter of Nutro, I'd like to share the following speech, given by the National Military Director, who spoke during David's retirement ceremony. This simple speech has a very profound message: "First you are here, and then you're not." It is a memorable and honorable way to close the final chapter of Nutro Products.

> In his commencement speech last year at Whitman College, Eric Idle, the star of Monty Python, said, "Life has a very simple plot: First you're here and then you're not." And so it seems to me that seventeen

years have gone by very quickly and with that so many friends past and present.

For those of you with whom I have worked most closely, I want to say thank you for your friendship and support . . . I want to say thank you for the opportunity you have given me to wake up every day with a sense of purpose and passion, and the chance to serve a cause greater than myself.

And for those of us who will report to work tomorrow morning at zero dark thirty, I ask that you do so joyfully, because retirement will come to each of us in our turn. It is not something to be rushed or encouraged, because it too brings its own set of challenges.

Therefore, I ask that you live each day mindfully and in appreciation of the gifts you have been given, for there are no guarantees of tomorrow, only today. So, when you leave here tonight, please remember this one thing: "Life has a very simple plot: First you're here, and then you're not."

The company changed ownership in May 2007 and has since undergone eight reorganizations—or "revitalizations," as the new management called it—giving the phrase "first you're here and then you're not" another level of meaning.

At the peak of Nutro's success, over 350 salespeople worked at the company—most across six national regions—plus a dozen members of the international team. When the company was purchased in 2009, Bob Gamgort, then-president of Mars, shared this about Nutro: "The sales team was the crown jewel. We bought the company to complete our portfolio and because of the sales team. We want to integrate Nutro into Mars and invigorate the passion the Nutro sales team has into Mars."

Beginning in 2009, with an economy in a recession and a re-evaluation of the hierarchy, the new ownership decided to reorganize Nutro Products. Eight years have passed and eight reorganizations have taken place. When we look around in the pet industry today, we notice that many of the people who work in it started with Nutro Products. Make no mistake; if you are "Legacy Nutro," you are still the "crown jewels." No matter where you are and where you go, we will always be a band of brothers!

AUTHOR'S NOTE: FACT OR FABLE?

"A people without the knowledge of their past history, origin and culture is like a tree without roots."

—Marcus Garvey

Historians consider what they do to be a real craft. They are not just excellent storytellers; they seek the truth by conducting impartial research. Once they introduce a new fact, most historians will record the information so future generations can learn from it. While history is the study of the past, it also helps to provide an identity for people or organizations. Of course, an identity sometimes becomes muddled over time—and it's up to current generations to seek out the facts of what happened to create a new and more accurate account of the actual events. As authors, we discovered both unrecorded and new facts when doing research for this book that differ from the original stories we—and many others—heard about Nutro. As such, the lineage of this documented story has three family trees to review.

Fable

According to company folklore, there are a few stores about how the company got started. One such story says John Saleen purchased the company in 1926 from a British entrepreneur, James Spratt, and relocated it from the United Kingdom to the United States. 33 As the story goes, Saleen then sold the company to Dave Traitel.

Another published story is from the *Nutro Products Professional Development Booklet* (1996), a manual given to all sales representatives and demonstrators hired by the company. This booklet references the company's history in the following way: "Branded packaged pet food is an English innovation dating to the late 1800s . . . an English family named Spratt was manufacturing dog food in the US. In 1926 they sold their equipment to a gentleman named John Saleen . . . [who] relocated to Los Angeles and formed Nutro Products, Inc." We uncovered further evidence via a video created by two company marketing gurus in 1989, which elaborates, "In 1895, Mr. Spratt brings his company to New York and later in the 1920s he built a second plant in San Francisco. Mr. Spratt decides he wants to go back to England and sells the rights to his dog food formula to John Saleen in 1926. John Saleen then becomes the founder of Nutro Dog Food Company."

This is where we want to address some facts—specifically, to note that James Spratt died circa 1880 and sold his company in 1878 to C.J. Wylam. Additionally, John Saleen was born in 1918 and passed away in 2002. This means that it is *impossible for James Spratt and John Saleen's paths to have crossed*. This fable was more of a romanticized tale—and probably just a cleaner story that the Nutro marketing department may have conjured up.

So what *really* happened, then?

Herben Serois Lineage
Fact

The first family tree is Herben Serois, a name people in the pet indus-try have never heard of. On September 1, 1931, Herben Serois started a small pet food company that he named the Nutro Dog Food Company. Contrary to the previously told romanticized story, *Herben* was the founder—not John Saleen, and certainly not James Spratt. Herben's business was located in the heart of Santa Monica, California. The Nutro trademark, approved in 1936, was to encompass dog food, cat food, and fox food. Herben ran his company until his death at age sixty-three in 1942. Little is recorded on Herben that we could find. Only his obituary, his grave marker (Forest Lawn Memorial in Glendale, California), the actual United States Patent Trade-Mark filing (Figure 27), and a few other historical facts mentioned in Chapter 4.

AFFIDAVIT SEC. 8
ACCEPTED
Registered May 12, 1936

AFFIDAVIT SEC. 15
RECEIVED 2-6-57

Trade-Mark 334,656

RENEWED

REPUBLISHED

Under Sec. 12 (c) 1946 Act JAN 15 1952

John C. Salem
d/b/a Nutro Dog Food Co.,
El Monte, Calif.

UNITED STATES PATENT OFFICE

Herben Serois, doing business as Nutro Dog Food
Company, Santa Monica, Calif.

Act of February 20, 1905

Application October 8, 1934, Serial No. 356,888

STATEMENT

To the Commissioner of Patents:

Herben Serois, a citizen of the United States of America, residing at Santa Monica, California, and doing business as Nutro Dog Food Company, at No. 1801-05 Fourteenth Street, Santa Monica, California, has adopted and used the trade-mark shown in the accompanying drawing, for DOG FOOD, CAT FOOD, AND FOX FOOD, in Class 46, Foods and ingredients of foods, and presents herewith five specimens showing the trade-mark as actually used by applicant upon the goods, and requests that the same be registered in the United States Patent Office in accordance with the act of February 20, 1905.

The trade-mark has been continuously used and applied to said goods in applicant's business since September 1, 1931.

The trade-mark is applied or affixed to the goods, or to the packages containing the same by printing the mark directly upon the containers of the goods or by applying labels bearing the mark directly to the containers.

The undersigned hereby appoints Martin P. Smith, whose postal address is 221 Consolidated Building, Los Angeles, California, registry No. 9,862, his attorney, to prosecute this application for registration, with full powers of substitution and revocation, and to make alterations and amendments therein, to receive the certificate, and to transact all business in the Patent Office connected therewith.

HERBEN SEROIS.

Figure 27: USPTO: Nutro Trademark.

Saleen Lineage

John Saleen (born in 1918) became the new owner of Nutro Dog Foods in approximately 1947. For the next two decades, John and his family operated the business locally in El Monte, California. But as discussed in Chapter 4, John's children did not have the same passion for running the family business as he did. Each of John's children began their careers, and John later agreed to sell his operation to Ed Brown, David Traitel, and a few other silent partners.

Over time, David Traitel bought out his partners and became the sole owner for many years. Eventually, Dave found himself in a similar position to John Saleen: His children did not want to run the family business. Finally, in 2006, Bain and Associates solidified a management-led buyout deal in obtaining Nutro Products for just a smidge over $1 billion. Just a few short years later, the company was set up to be acquired by Mars, Inc.—and purchased for $2.1 billion. Not a bad investment!

James Spratt Lineage

Most people would agree that James Spratt is the founding father of commercial dog food. But little is known about Spratt, and gaining historical information on this elusive man has been challenging. We know that he was born in Ohio and relocated to the United Kingdom around 1850 for varying reasons. James invented many items, and had patents for electrical lightning conductors—which is what most authors publish about him. His legendary Fibrine Meat Dog Cakes is what has given Spratt his notoriety in the pet food industry.

Spratt formed his company in 1860, and just a few years before his death (circa 1880), he sold it to Edward Wylam. In 1885, Edward Wylam added two partners, CJ Wylam and Beetham Batcheor, who invested a combined £200,000. Soon thereafter, the company went public under the name Spratt's Patent Ltd. After being incorporated, the operation moved to New York in 1895—with other offices in Newark, New Jersey.

After Spratt's death, his company's lineage continued in England and the United States, where it also gained new distribution. In 1950, General Mills purchased Spratt's Patent Ltd.; in 1961, Spillers acquired the company and initiated a few name changes. In 1968, they called it Spratt's Patent Holdings; then changed it again in 1972 to Spillers Food Ltd. Nestle then acquired Spillers for £715 million. Finally, in 2004, Spratt's Patent Ltd. was finally laid to rest and dissolved.

As authors and quasi-historians, we share these three family trees to reveal the actual accounting of ownership and a historical timeline. The story muddled over time is the ownership of Nutro. We assumed that those not in the pet industry or having no known prior affiliation or knowledge of Nutro would not at first glance appreciate this significance. The story of the company's beginning that has been told over time goes like this:

1. Nutro began in 1926.

2. John Saleen bought the company from James Spratt, a British entrepreneur.

3. John later sold the company.

Contrary to popular belief, though, James Spratt never owned Nutro, never brought the company to the US, and never sold it to John Saleen. Mathematically, this timeline does not add up. James Spratt passed away circa 1880 and John Saleen was born in 1918. Their paths never crossed.

While the Spratt company did come to the US, James was not the one who brought it. We must therefore give credit for Nutro's humble beginnings to Herben Serois—a name that, until now, had been virtually ignored in the history of pet food.

Herben Serois applied for a trademark on October 8, 1934, which was later approved in 1936. He died in 1942, and his company was sold to the Saleen family. Herman ran the business along with his homemade meatloaf for dogs and foxes. Mike Saleen recounts, "Sometime around

1947, my father purchased the Nutro Dog Food Company from his Uncle [Herman]." John owned the company until he sold it to Ed Brown and David Traitel in 1976. The company was later sold to Bain and Associates in a management-led acquisition.

It is currently owned by Mars Incorporated and has been since May 2007.

APPENDIX A

The 10 Nutro Consumer Commandments

Author and Source: Dewey Long

A wise man and visionary, Dave Traitel was tempted by the low-hanging fruit in the garden of feedin'. In the third month of our year 1985, Max was created. And it was good. Formulated for skin and coat, and unlike those that came before, it was not born of bone or guts, but from meal gathered from the finest shepherds in the land. Chicken, lamb, and rice had never been heard of before. The product differentiated from others by these ingredients had a story that needed to be told. Mr. Traitel summoned his disciple, Ladd Hardy, to load up the Max two-by-two into his station wagon and head to the promised land of Burbank, California.

People came from all around to see the product, hear the story, and be converted. To further spread the word, comparative charts were placed throughout the land so that all may learn and benefit from their teachings.

Max was undeniably the best pet food in the world. The problem was how to get the message—The Nutro Story—out to all the people. Should we follow our predecessors down the path of no growth ruin—via television, radio, magazines, and newspaper? These evil media, so detached from personal contact, were not the answer. Most pet food purchases are made from recommendation. How, then, do we gain that recommendation?

Although all pet food peddlers say the same things about palatability, digestibility, stool volume, skin, and coat, no one can say their food outperforms Nutro. Better performance through better ingredients—*that* is the Nutro difference.

To tell this story and gain recommendation, we must go forth and multiply ourselves through other people. By building lasting relationships through trust, integrity, and accountability. How do we build that trust and that relationship? Think consumer. Let's talk about the 10 Consumer Commandments that each Nutro pet food peddler must know:

1. Thou shalt know thy product and its benefits and why it is different.

2. Empathize with the customer. Help them understand how Nutro Products can solve their problems.

3. Be organized and efficient—time is precious.

4. Be prompt. Quick response earns respect.

5. Follow-through builds loyalty.

6. Provide solutions. Anyone can define a problem. Successful people provide solutions.

7. Be on time. Don't miss your opportunity.

8. Work hard. Keep your customers satisfied.

9. Be enthusiastic. It is contagious.

10. Be honest.

ABOUT THE AUTHORS

Christie Cooper is the current president of Cooper Consulting Group. Previously she worked at The Nutro Company for eighteen years in a variety of roles, including regional manager of national accounts and independent territory manager. She worked in the training department for seven years, alongside the director of training. While conducting training at Nutro, she found her true passion, which contributed to her vision: to "inspire learning and leadership development to help leaders and teams be their best."

Christie has her doctorate degree in education with an emphasis in organizational leadership from Pepperdine University. Christie has been married to Howard for thirty-one years and together they have a daughter, Lauren, who works in the pet food industry. Christie maintains her competitive spirit by showing and competing in dressage at the FEI levels.

Mary Hooks was employed with Nutro for her entire adult career. She started out as a demonstrator working short shifts with key retailers. She had many other roles that contributed to the significant growth at Nutro. She left the business in 2014 and currently enjoys her free time with her two grown girls, Meagan and Ashley, and her granddaughter, Ellie. Mary was born in Encino, California, on May 26, and has three brothers— Ed, David, and Gavin—and a sister, Pam. Currently, she resides in Coeur d' Alene, Idaho, with her husband, Steve, of thirty-four years, and their Golden Doodle, Chuy.

Mary enjoys the adventure of life. She wakes up every day thankful for each new beautiful day with her friends and family. Mary struggled with dyslexia during high school and now serves as a role model to others by overcoming this challenge and having a successful career at Nutro.

FURTHER READING AND RESOURCES

(Endnotes)

1. Preview of Prominent Families of New Jersey: in Two Volumes

2. http://www.rmg.co.uk/discover/explore/ships-biscuit

3. Preview of Prominent Families of New Jersey: in Two Volumes, page 667

4. Scrapes and Spratts to Specialty Diets; Caroline Coile, Ph.D. AKC Gasette; September 2009; 126, 9: Research Library page 18.

5. Grace's Guide to British Industrial History: http://www.graces-guide.co.uk/Spratt's_Patent

6. http://ntp.niehs.nih.gov/ntp/roc/content/profiles/butylatedhy-droxyanisole.pdf

7. http://www.gallup.com/poll/25969/Americans-Their-Pets.aspx

8. http://www.l3corp.net/2012/robert-moran-ceo-of-petsmart-inc-on-how-the-family-dog-has-become-a-family-member/

9. http://www.bls.gov/opub/btn/volume-2/spending-on-pets.htm

10. http://www.petfoodindus-try.com/blogs/7-adventures-in-pet-food/post/5609-global-pet-food-trends-sales-and-volume-rose-4-in-2015

11. http://www.ecology.com/birth-death-rates/

12. https://www.avma.org/KB/Resources/Statistics/Pages/Market-research-statistics-US-pet-ownership.aspx

13. http://www.reuters.com/article/us-mars-pgpetcare-acquisition-idUSBREA3811O20140409

14. Mathile, Clayton Dream No Little Dreams DNLD Publishing;

15. https://faunalytics.org/feature-article/most-pet-owners-will-spend-anything-to-save-pets-life-survey-says/

16. https://faunalytics.org/feature-article/2011-2012-appa-national-pet-owners-survey/

17. https://faunalytics.org/wp-content/uploads/2015/05/Citation1338.pdf

18. http://www.census.gov/const/uspricemon

19. http://www.infoplease.com/ipa/A0774473.html

20. http://www.jimcollins.com/article_topics/articles/hitting-the-wall.html#articletop

21. http://publications.americanalpineclub.org/articles/12197912200/print

22. Marshall Goldsmith: Mojo

23. https://www.psychologytoday.com/articles/199707/finding-flow

24. Organizational Culture and Leadership (1994) Page 12, 4th Edition- Edgar H.

25. Work Role Ambiguity, Job Satisfaction and Job Performance: Meta-Analyses and Review. D. Abramis, December 1, 1994; Psychological Reports, 75, 1411-1433.

26. https://www.zapposinsights.com/culture-book/digital-version/download-cb

27. https://corporateofficehq.com/petsmart-corporate-office/

28. http://www.retailcustomerexperience.com/blogs/how-smart-is-petsmart/ Annamarie Turano

29. https://corporateofficehq.com/petsmart-corporate-office/

30. McKinsey & Company: Unlocking the full potential of women at work. Joanna Barsh and Lareina Yee

31. 2013 Digital Transformation Global Executive Study and Research Project

32. Nielsen Global Track Complete Sales Value and Industry Coverage Matrix